On Love

On Love

A Philosophy for the Twenty-First Century

Luc Ferry

Translated by Andrew Brown

polity

First published in French as *De l'amour* © Editions Odile Jacob, 2012

This English edition © Polity Press, 2013

Polity Press
65 Bridge Street
Cambridge CB2 1UR, UK

Polity Press
350 Main Street
Malden, MA 02148, USA

ISBN-13: 978-0-7456-7017-1

A catalogue record for this book is available from the British Library.

Typeset in 11 on 13 pt Sabon
by Toppan Best-set Premedia Limited
Printed and bound in Great Britain by the MPG Printgroup

The publisher has used its best endeavours to ensure that the URLs for external websites referred to in this book are correct and active at the time of going to press. However, the publisher has no responsibility for the websites and can make no guarantee that a site will remain live or that the content is or will remain appropriate.

For further information on Polity, visit our website: www.politybooks.com

Contents

Preface

The global crisis in which we find ourselves enmeshed has intensified the feeling that the world is out of control, that political remedies, on the Right and on the Left, no longer have any purchase on reality, that the values in whose name we act apply less and less to our way of life. We cannot continue to give in to this schizophrenia, this bad faith that makes us think of the present in terms of yesterday's ideas – ideas that are now clearly obsolete. The aim of this book is, firstly, to show how and why this long period of bewilderment is producing, without our yet being fully aware of it, a new principle of meaning that will enable us to regain control over our destinies, give coherence to our way of seeing the world and set up ideals we can believe in; and secondly, it seeks to analyse the profound concrete changes that result from it in the great domains of individual and collective existence, namely, the family, politics, education and art.

The public discourse of republican values (values that are no longer an issue in the debate, since we all support them, from the extreme Right to the extreme Left) is now light years away from the real questions of our lives as we see them (our children's futures, the most important man or woman in our lives, the coming of a society that will enable everyone to flourish freely). Hence the sterile stand-off between, on the one side, governments churning out endless measures that are doubtless technically or tactically justified, but whose overall aim is clear to nobody; and, on the other side, the anger, fear and indignation that have gripped ordinary people in so many countries.

It would be ungracious to lay the blame at the feet of politicians alone since each of us is prey to the same symptoms. Like them, we defend principles that no longer correspond to the way we act. The same people who protest every day against the snare and delusion of consumption will change their iPhones every six months; those who think we ought to go back to the old grey smocks that all French children used to wear still let their children post images of themselves in skimpy clothes on Facebook; and everyone swears by what is 'eco-friendly', but still owns a four-wheel drive – and there's nothing very fair about that. This is called 'accepting one's contradictions', a haughty way of saying that we are accepting nothing except our inability to choose ideals that we really agree with. In short, our representations no longer match up to the truth of our intimate experience; and this consigns us all to the position of 'do as I say, not as I do'.

How can this divorce be explained? For over a century and a half, the arts, philosophy and our lifestyles have continued to liberate and then give value to hitherto forgotten, marginalized or repressed dimensions of human existence: to sexuality, the unconscious, the feminine element in men and the masculine element in women; to childhood, and our animal and natural aspects. Baudelaire was not the first to have been 'as bored as a dead rat', but he was the first to turn this into art, to reveal all the wealth, the authenticity, the freedom of imagination that can unfold in these moments of 'spleen'. In this way, he opened up a domain to which we are all heirs. From Philippe Delerm's *The Small Pleasures of Life* to Bénabar's songs, from a weekend at Center Parcs to the 'right not to be a perfect mother', we never cease recycling his work, for good and ill. As a result of this movement, paradoxically taken up and amplified by global capitalism even though it originally claimed to be radically anti-bourgeois, private values have become the main source of public values. All the great ideals that gave life meaning (God, one's country, the Revolution) are now in a fragile state in Europe; love is henceforth the only value in which we all unreservedly believe. This is why education, health, assistance for dependants, the preservation of the planet for future generations and, more generally, all the initiatives designed to foster the full realization of each person have become central themes in the political debate.

But the problem is that the main frameworks at our disposal for understanding collective life do not take into account this now decisive aspect of our existences. Liberalism is no better than socialism or nationalism at integrating private life into the dynamics of public life. Indeed, they do the complete opposite: they reject it from the political sphere on principle. Of course, this was originally done out of a still legitimate concern to guarantee the full autonomy of the private sphere by taking it out of the illegitimate control of public powers. Today, however, it is the opposite movement that needs to be given its due place since it is clear that a growing number of collective issues arise from new common expectations deeply rooted in the convergence of individual aspirations. This means we need to acknowledge that we were mistaken to limit politics just to the managing of interests: in fact, passions have always played a decisive role in it. A reading of Shakespeare should have been enough to make us realize this.

In other words, we are in one of those rare but decisive transitional periods when our frameworks of understanding, our now outdated cultural markers, no longer enable us to find our way through events as they happen, and even less guide these events effectively. This calls for an in-depth metamorphosis in the way we envisage our lives.

When I met Luc Ferry, over twenty years ago, we immediately ... had a huge row! About pretty much everything: modern art, education, politics .... I was dead set on giving their full meaning to the new forms of existence that now lie at the heart of our lives, while his main concern was first of all to integrate these new aspects into a 'non-metaphysical' reformulation of humanism that would preserve their definitive contributions. In any event, we agreed that we couldn't leave things there and that the available philosophies were no longer adequate, either because they were immediately vulnerable to the objections of Nietzsche and his successors, or because they led to a permanent double discourse that consisted, for example, in radically criticizing the idea that there are universal moral values while calling one's neighbour a bastard in the name of these same values.

Since that time we have become the best of friends. Over thousands of hours of discussion, I have gradually seen a philosophy take shape – one that, if I may speak as I find, makes it possible not just for our differences to be overcome, but above all for an answer to be given to our need for a way of thinking that will really shed light on the present world and the very kernel of the lives we live in it. Since neither of us was in bad faith, the human experiences on which we based our arguments all had some truth in them. From then on, the aim of the conversation was not to win out over the other by having the 'final word' in the argument but to understand the reason for our differences of opinion.

I now feel that, in his latest books, Luc Ferry has succeeded in developing an altogether original philosophy based on a new principle that gives us a much more direct and profound access to the experience of the world that is now ours. For the first time in decades, or even a whole century, he has laid a foundation and a way of building on it which will enable us to construct a real philosophical system, in other words a way of giving a proper coherence to the diversity of our experiences, and thus of endowing our lives with overall meaning.

Of course, you can always retort that you're a pragmatist and that you won't have anything to do with 'ideas': after all, why not? And yet, there is nothing more illusory than this affectation of pure realism: experience proves that those who claim that they are happy to stop there are nonetheless forever telling us 'what we need to think' about things. The only difference is that they serve up stale 'received ideas' which, as we have seen, have nothing very fruitful to say to us anymore. Unlike what many people imagine, philosophy is not of use to philosophers alone, or even mainly. When Descartes constructed a philosophy based on 'common sense' alone, 'the most widely shared thing in the world', and on the well-known words 'I think, therefore I am', he provided us with a framework which, right up to the French Revolution, liberated whole generations whose ancestors had long been at a loss about whether to follow the commands of the Church, those of the prince, the thoughts of Aristotle, the demands of tradition, the wishes of their fathers, or their own free will: you need only read the plays of Molière to see how the characters' love affairs can be hampered by conflicts of legitimacy. In this sense, everyone has benefited from Descartes, even those who haven't read him! In the nineteenth century, the limits of the purely rational and moral vision of the world that had led the French

Revolution to a complete dead end forced philosophers to reintegrate forgotten dimensions of human life within its purview:
history in Hegel, class struggle linked to relations of production
in Marx, the will to power and the unconscious in Nietzsche.

It is a comparable revolution which Luc Ferry is proposing
to us. But in my view this new philosophy has not previously
appeared in its fullest guise, partly because the author, for pedagogic reasons, has given a great deal of room to several other
philosophers, partly because he needed to give his ideas a firm
foundation by drawing on various analyses (historical, anthropological, conceptual). Probably, too, the very idea that one has put
one's finger on the long-awaited solution inclines one to caution
and to a certain discretion in the presentation of one's discovery.

The project of this book, indeed, is to try and set out, as clearly
as possible (this time without any side tracks or false modesty)
this new philosophy that we so much need, and to show how it
will help us better to find our way in this world of ours, in the
most concrete areas of activity. Like all true philosophies, it is not
in the least some fanciful idea pulled out of thin air to be imposed
on the more credulous among us. Rather, it is an effort to focus
on what drives us all at the deepest level – something for which
we hitherto did not have the words, or any adequate vision.

Claude Capelier

Introduction: A Brief History
of the Meaning of Life

Luc Ferry: First, a few words on the title I've chosen for this book. Why this homage to Stendhal? Of course, I was initially wary of reusing his title *On Love* (*De l'amour*). I was worried that such a borrowing might seem too pretentious, since he placed the bar so high. Of course, the title should be taken as the expression of a debt of admiration, as a homage to Stendhal's confession, which I find so deeply moving and with which I can identify so closely: 'Love has always been, for me, the greatest thing of all ... or rather, the *only* thing!' What Stendhal means is that love isn't just one feeling among others, a common passion like other passions such as fear, anger, jealousy or indignation. It's a new principle of meaning, a principle that shapes a completely new conception of the good life: it inaugurates a new era in the history of thought and of life, as I shall be attempting to show over the following pages.

Although love is, no doubt, as old as humanity, and although it is always ambiguous, being accompanied by its opposite (hatred), its emergence within the modern family – in other words the shift from arranged marriage (or marriage of convenience) to marriage chosen freely through and for the flourishing of love (especially the love of children) – has changed the tenor of our lives, and not just in the private sphere. Art and politics have also been profoundly altered by this change, and it is the impact of these revolutions in private life on the public sphere that I would like to explore in this essay. This is why, in spite of my initial hesitations, I finally decided that *On Love* was the only possible title for this book.

I must warn our readers that we will not really be analysing this new principle of meaning, and – as they say – 'talking about love' straight away, but only in the first chapter that follows this introduction. Then, in the second chapter, I'd like us to discuss how this new principle is going to bring about a radical change at the most collective and most public level of all, namely politics, so as to drive home the lesson that we're not just talking about the history of private life. Finally, within the same framework, we'll be talking about art and education.

But in this introduction, the first task is to give a quick overview of the historical dynamic and the human problems that make this change of paradigm necessary. We can't avoid this preliminary stage if we are to gain a proper understanding of what is entailed by the idea of a 'new principle of meaning', 'a new definition of the good life' that requires a completely new kind of philosophical thinking. This is why, by way of preamble, I would like to do something I've not really done before and highlight the connection between the two main themes that I have discussed in my previous books. On the one hand, there's the definition of philosophy as the quest for the good life, for wisdom or for a secular spirituality – in other words, the idea that (like religion) philosophy strives to define a blessed life for us mortals, but without going via God or faith. And on the other hand, there is what I've called the 'revolution of love' that accompanies the shift, in modern Europe, from arranged marriage and the traditional family to marrying for love as it underlies today's family life.

In my view, these two themes are inseparable in so far as the second theme, which implies a formidable rise in the influence of love as the organizing principle of our lives, necessitates – on the philosophical and not just existential level – a new definition of the good life, of the meaning of life, and of the wisdom required if one is to attain it. Obviously, the history of private life was bound to have an impact on collective, public, and even political life, and it is mainly this which I would like to analyse here. As we shall see, this way of thinking marks such a break from traditional political systems that it is still difficult to discern. The liberal tradition, like the socialist tradition – the two lines of thought and action that have dominated the history of modern Europe ever since the French Revolution – have shared two major features. First, they both relegated everything that belonged to the private sphere and 'civil society' to a realm that lay outside the field of noble politics. Second, they considered politics merely as a way of managing private interests in the name of the general interest, whereas – as I will be showing – passions often play a much more predominant role in history than do interests as such.

We'll be coming back to this. But let's start by summarizing, albeit briefly, the main guideline of my philosophical thinking.

First guideline: a definition of philosophy as the non-religious quest for the good life

I've already set out this theme quite clearly in my book *Learning to Live*. Philosophy is actually quite different from the way it is usually presented in the final year of French secondary schools. The pedagogic literature on philosophy teaching tends to see it as no more than a general art of argument, a sort of 'method of thinking', a training in 'critical thought' which would ideally aim at getting pupils to 'think for themselves', to become more independent, by doing exercises such as writing essays or commentaries on texts. Of course, I'm not in the least averse to this kind of focus. Indeed, it's an excellent plan. It's just that it falls more within the scope of an intelligent civic education than within philosophy as such – to which it is only very distantly connected. If anyone had told Plato, Epicurus, Spinoza or Nietzsche that they were philosophizing in order to write 'essays' or to 'learn how to think properly', I reckon they'd have simply roared with laughter! *Philo-sophia*: etymologically, 'quest for' or 'love of' 'wisdom' – the word had a meaning for them, as we can see even in Nietzsche, in aphorisms such as the one entitled 'Why I am so wise' ...

What I wanted to show, in *Learning to Live*, was this: throughout the philosophical tradition from the ancient world up to Heidegger, by way of Spinoza, Lucretius, Kant and Nietzsche, philosophy was always conceived – at least by the greatest thinkers, without any exception – as the attempt to define the good life, the highest good, the blessed life and the wisdom that leads to it:

in short, as an attempt to answer the great question of what the meaning of life can be for mortals. This is what I have called a secular spirituality and a doctrine of salvation without God. Why? Because, unlike the great religions, and even though they have the same aim in view (identifying the conditions of a good life for those who are doomed to die), philosophy really does try to provide its own definition of the ultimate meaning of our lives, without going through God, without going through faith.

I'm sometimes told that there is no such meaning, that the concept of 'the meaning of life' is meaningless, except from a religious point of view, since it would require us to stand outside life, so to speak, if we are to give it a purpose – and this is possible only for believers. Maybe. This objection, however, is based on a piece of sophistry that it would be pointless to dwell on too long. Let's just say, so as to remove any doubts that might trouble my readers, that *in all the major philosophies it's a question of asking what is meaningful* within *our lives*, what may comprise their final purpose when seen from within. Spinoza, for example – and we can't suspect *him* of yielding to any illusions about a meaning that transcends life – never stops insisting on this: there is a final aim that human beings can set up for themselves thanks to philosophy, and this aim is salvation and joy, obtained through wisdom and understanding. He says the same thing in the very last lines of the *Ethics*, where we find him convinced that he has shown the true paths that lead to a blessed life for all humans willing to follow them. Unlike the ignorant person, who has not read the *Ethics* or gone through the stages that lead to a true understanding of things, the truly wise person

> is hardly troubled in spirit, but being, by a certain eternal necessity, conscious of himself, and of God, and of things, he never ceases to be, but always possesses true peace of mind. If the way I have shown to lead to these things now seems very hard, it can still be found. And of course, what is found so rarely must be hard. For if salvation were at hand, and could be found without great effort, how could nearly everyone neglect it? But all things excellent are as difficult as they are rare. (Part V, prop. 42, scholium, tr. Edwin Curley)

Here we see that, for Spinoza – but he is expressing a conviction shared by all great philosophers – philosophy can be reduced neither to 'thinking well', nor even to the idea of autonomy. These two qualities are of course required for it, but they are merely necessary, and not sufficient, conditions for philosophizing properly. For in the final analysis, philosophy is indeed, not an art of eloquence, but a doctrine of secular salvation, a wisdom without God, or at least without God as understood in the great monotheistic religions, and without the succour of faith, since it is through the lucidity of reason, with the means we have to hand, that we are to attain real wisdom. So here we have a meaning, a purpose assigned by philosophy to human life.

As a great historian of the ancient world, the late Pierre Hadot, has shown, in the philosophical schools of Ancient Greece, the aim was not learning to wax eloquent about general concepts or to put together school essays with beginnings, middles and ends: it was learning to live, to attain wisdom. Hence the exercises that were imposed on disciples, among the Stoics, for example. I've often mentioned the case of the dead fish which the disciples of Zeno, the founder of the Stoic school, were requested to drag around on a leash in the market square in Athens. What was the aim of this strange exercise in wisdom? It was to learn to disdain what other people might say, the 'bourgeois' conventions, and turn one's gaze to the truth, which, after all, disdains artificial rules. To attain the good life, it's no doubt better to think properly, but we also need to *live* our thoughts, not to stay at the level of theory alone.

This theme is also found in Schopenhauer, even though he can be considered the founder of contemporary thought: in spite of the 'pessimism' which is all that hasty and superficial readers see in him, the aim of his philosophy is mainly to get through the stage of learning how to think and to attain the good life by following the principles of an 'art of happiness', a 'eudaimonic art' – titles which Schopenhauer himself had chosen to organize his last thoughts.

Of course, in every great philosophy there is also a theoretical part (generally known as the 'theory of knowledge') and a 'practical' part (which concerns ethics and politics). Our traditional school textbooks used to be generally divided into two volumes: 'Knowledge' and 'Action'. The doctrine of wisdom or of salvation without God properly speaking is, of course, merely the final stage of philosophy, its ultimate or higher end, so to speak and it, as it were, crowns two other areas whose importance I really don't want to underestimate. *First, there is a theoretical part*, generally known as the 'theory of knowledge', in which are found the various attempts (empiricist, idealist, criticist or phenomenological, for example) to explain our human ability to forge objective representations of the world and our experience. This is obviously an essential part of philosophy, as I would be the first to admit. The fact remains that this theoretical aspect is always connected with the question of wisdom, of the good life: this is indeed what distinguishes philosophical theories from scientific theories. Of course, the point is to understand the world, to form an idea or representation of it, and the great philosophers make use of the scientific knowledge available in their time (in astronomy, biology, physics, etc.) in order to do so. Despite what is sometimes said, most of the great philosophers of the past tended to be good scientists, or at least they were well informed about the science of their time. And it is worth noting that their theories of knowledge considered the sciences from an original standpoint: it was less a matter of knowing this or that sector of the real, the living things studied by biology, forces and matter in physics, planets in astronomy, and so on, than of trying to create *an overall image of the world as the playing field of human life*, i.e., as the field in which our existence has to take place: is this world knowable or mysterious, favourable or hostile, beautiful or ugly, harmonious or chaotic – how can we know it, and so on? These were the questions raised by ancient philosophy: they are quite clearly different from individual scientific inquiries. Thus, as is very clear in the case of the Stoics and Epicureans, there is always a connection – even in the most theoretical part of philosophy – with the central question of what a good life for mortals might be. Pierre Hadot brought out extremely clearly how decisive this preoccupation was in the theories put forward by the philosophers of antiquity. Even in the theoretical part, the world is not analysed from an absolutely objective point of view in the way a scientist would see it. Even less is it a matter of analysing one part of the world, in the way a biologist focuses on life, a sociologist on society or a physicist on matter or energy. The philosopher is different: he or she tries to draw on all the knowledge available so as to form a general representation of the world. This again shows that what is crucial is the world seen from a 'soteriological' point of view (the quest for salvation) or from an ethical standpoint: the world as the playing field of human life.

After the theoretical part, there is, in every great philosophy, a practical part. The importance of this is also something I have no wish to minimize: it includes ethical and political philosophy. Basically, *the preoccupation of ethics* is not the playing field itself, but *the rules of the game which are to govern the dynamics of life as played out between human beings*. How can humans and their relationships be pacified when they are free and thus tempted by egotism, by conflict, by anger? There again, when we look at the great theories of ethics since the birth of western philosophy in Greece, we soon realize that they too are always connected to the third dimension of philosophy that I call 'the question of the good life', the question of wisdom and spirituality.

Now these two parts of philosophy, whose importance I wouldn't dream of denying, gain meaning only when related to a third 'level', which I analysed in *Learning to Live* and which again corresponds to the question of the good life, wisdom, the *meaning of life* – expressions which should here be understood as equivalent. In every case, we need to define what *gives meaning* to our lives, in other words to grasp what in the final analysis motivates our actions and justifies, as it were, our lives, sometimes without our even being aware of it – the 'background motivation', we might say. This is the first main guideline and I'd now like to link it to the second.

Second guideline: how love finally became the main source of the meaning of our lives

The second guideline is the one that lies at the heart of my book *La Révolution de l'amour* (*The Revolution of Love*). It is based on an analysis that may initially appear somewhat historical, but which in reality is essentially philosophical. However, nobody philosophizes on just anything, simply to wax eloquent about general concepts. We philosophize about the real, and in this respect it's always seemed crucial to me to root philosophical thinking in the natural sciences as well as in the sciences of history. My approach to the 'revolution of love' happens to be based first and foremost on the indispensable and enthralling work of

historians such as Philippe Ariès, to whom I pay homage, as well
as Jean-Louis Flandrin, Edward Shorter, John Boswell and François
Lebrun, all of whom gave us new ways of thinking about daily
life in ancient times. They founded what is called the 'history of
mentalities' or 'the new history'. Instead of concentrating on great
battles, diplomacy between states or social classes – all of them
fundamentally 'grandiose' themes – they dwelt on the warp and
weft of the day-to-day life of ordinary individuals in bygone
periods: what they ate, how they died, how they educated their
children, how they got married, what sort of families they had ...
In the light of the new horizons opened up by these historians, I
have taken a great interest in what, in my view, appears as the
main source for the great revolution which our lives are currently
undergoing: the shift from the 'marriage of convenience', the
arranged marriage (arranged not just by parents but by villages),
to the marriage chosen by young people based on, and for the
sake of, love. 'For the sake of love' means for the flourishing of
love in the family, the love of children and, more widely, the bond
between generations.

This shift from the 'marriage of convenience', the basis of the
traditional family, to marrying for love and the modern family,
was a long process that took several centuries. It began in
the seventeenth century – we can see its traces in the plays of
Molière where, already, the children are rebelling against parents
who want to marry them off 'by force'. But it was only after the
Second World War that this new model became universal, first in
Europe, then, to a greater or lesser extent, in the other parts of
the world.

Meanwhile, and this is an essential point, the advent of love as
the sole legitimate basis for couples and families soon went beyond
the framework of marriage and became the rule in all loving
unions, whether the people involved were married or not, whether
or not they were of the same sex. The demand for gay marriage
is, in this sense, the endpoint of this history in its attempt to separate the idea of a union of couples from its traditional principles:
lineage, biology, economy. Even in my childhood, it was still
extremely rare, in bourgeois milieus, for anyone to get married
without their father's consent: there were obvious economic, social
and inheritance reasons for this. 'Morganatic' marriages, unions
in which the economic and social differences would have been too

marked, were avoided. As for homosexual unions, based solely on the 'right to love', outside any consideration of biology or lineage, there was no question of them – not even in people's dreams! These traditional visions, of course, still linger on, but they are gradually fading away and, at least in principle, everyone tends to acknowledge that in this old Europe of ours, love – and I might even say romantic love (since, as we shall see, there are quite clearly several sorts of love) – has become the main principle behind our unions. It is a magnificent but often problematic principle: basing family life on romantic love also means, as we need to make clear from the start, basing it on terribly fragile and shifting ground. Romantic love, as everyone knows (or should know) lasts for only a few years. After, if the couple wishes to survive the disappearance of this love, they will need to transform it into something more stable, a love that is not submitted to but one that is chosen, constructed, developed. A loving friendship, for instance, that will be able to last. The conversion from one form of love to the other is no easy matter, as witness the obvious fact that our loving unions last only for a while: 60 per cent of love marriages these days end up in divorce.

In this respect, we should point out straight away that, while love gives meaning to our lives, it does not always make them any easier. The next step is to claim that marrying for love has failed: but this is a step that I don't want to take. What woman – what man, even – would nowadays wish to go back to the marriage of convenience, arranged by parents and villages? I will let everyone give their own answer but, as far as I can see, it's perfectly clear: in spite of all the difficulties it arouses, a loving union is now the only one that appears to us, quite simply, worth having – and this, as I must emphasize, was not at all the case in bygone centuries.

The revolution of love has a profound impact on our ideas about the meaning of our lives: it requires a new philosophy

While philosophy culminates in a 'doctrine of salvation', highlighting the things that can give meaning to our lives in spite of death, the 'enthronement of love' that we continue to witness is modifying our perspectives and requires a new philosophy. This is what has led me, as I mentioned earlier, to establish for the first time an explicit link between these two themes: philosophy understood, on the one hand, not as an argument or a form of critical thinking, but as a quest for the good life; and, on the other hand, the revolution of love that will entail a new idea of the meaning of life in our societies, an unprecedented questioning that breaks away from the old definitions. What interests me, and what I would like to develop more concretely in this book, is the way in which this revolution will have a profound impact on our lives in the private sphere but also in everything that is linked to collective issues and the political arena. The aim of this book, in fact, is to try and provide a key to the impact this revolution will have and to discern its consequences for the main aspects of our individual and social lives.

Far from affecting the private sphere alone, the revolution of love profoundly modifies public issues

As I've just suggested, the mistake that continues to be made by the great political traditions in France, liberalism on the one side and socialism or communism on the other, consists in considering that revolutions in private life affect, or should affect, just the private sphere so that, basically speaking, politics can concern itself with the general interest alone, understood as the regulation of particular interests. In reality, this revolution of love, however intimate the feeling on which it is based may be, will transform every domain in human activity, including the most collective areas.

This is what I'd like us to discuss since in my view there is no substitute for discussion when one wishes to explore a new and as yet uncharted dimension of human experience. Not that love as such is new, of course, and I emphasize this so as to avoid a too frequent misunderstanding: love, no doubt, is as old as humanity – as is hatred. But love had never formed the basis, the unique and absolute organizing principle, behind the family cell as it began to do in modern Europe from the nineteenth century onwards. This was the new phenomenon, one which – if I may repeat myself – would only really take wing in the second half of the twentieth century, mainly in the western world (the marriage of convenience largely remained the rule in many civilizations outside Europe). How will this revolution of love simultaneously provide us with a new definition of the good life in its properly philosophical aspect and, on another level, entail fundamental transformations in the domains of education, art and politics? These are the questions that I would like us to tackle.

I am fully aware of the difficulty of the enterprise. It's always problematic to try and get people to understand such a radical change, a basic transformation which alters our usual representations in so many different ways, especially in the domain of politics. But the stakes are, in my view, so high that no effort should be spared in the attempt. So the aim of this book can be summed up clearly by saying that we need to focus on these two points: in what way does love comprise a new principle of meaning, and in what way does it modify our usual conceptions of education, art and politics?

Why the philosophies of the past can no longer satisfy us

Claude Capelier: In order to provide a clear answer to these two questions, we first need to explain why the definitions of the good life given by the great philosophers of the past – even though they still speak to us in so many ways – no longer manage to gain our assent: we've stopped believing in them, they seem to us to be light years away from our aspirations and the world in which we live.

Luc Ferry: In the history of western thought (though not only that), *four great principles of meaning, before that of love*, dominated bygone ages. It's crucial to understand how and why these great and ancient principles, although they continue to illuminate whole swathes of our experience, no longer strike us as credible reference points for guiding our thoughts and deeds. There is a paradox here, one which lies at the heart of the history of philosophy: the old principles of meaning *still speak to us* but, at the same time, *they no longer tell us* anything really decisive. They touch us, we sometimes find them grandiose, and indeed some people decide to 'live in' them – and yet, we can't help finding them to be in some way definitively relegated to the past, disconnected from our present-day lives. To give you one example from outside philosophy, a person can have a deep love for the music of Bach and, at the same time, realize that it belongs to a time that's no longer ours. This isn't an objection, of course, but this situation deserves to be pondered and it is found in analogous form in the history of philosophy.

Four great principles of meaning have, in succession, preceded the revolution of love

How can we give a brief sketch of these four great principles of meaning, in other words, these four great definitions of the good life, wisdom, or salvation without God (to say it yet again, these formulations are, in my view, synonymous), which preceded the revolution of love which we are now witnessing and participating in? What explains the relative obsolescence of a particular principle over the course of history and the emergence of a new paradigm?

The cosmological principle

The *first of these principles* appears with the *Odyssey* of Homer and the tale of Odysseus' travels: if you like, this is the *cosmic* or *cosmological* principle. To put it more clearly: the aim of human life, the purpose of Odysseus' adventures, is to travel from the initial chaos to a reconciliation with the harmony of the cosmos. Odysseus moves from war (the celebrated Trojan War) to peace, from chaos to harmony, from exile far from Ithaca, the state of which he is king, to a return 'home'. In the Greek conception of a hierarchical world in which everyone, in accordance with his degree of excellence, has his place assigned to him, being torn away from this 'natural place' is a form of suffering and injustice, just as a return home is a positive good connected with the restoration of the harmony of the cosmos. Odysseus is a king who has to leave his kingdom and his wife Penelope to take part in a savage war: this separation plunges him into a chaos that lasts twenty years. He takes ten years to win the war and another ten to return home. Now he is forever seeking harmony, reconciliation with the world: he seeks to find the place he has lost in the cosmic order. He's rather like the little cat or dog that you sometimes read about in the press at the end of summer, which got lost on the motorway and had to cover vast distances to get back home. Odysseus is like a little animal that's lost its 'natural place'; and he'll take twenty years to get back to his family in Ithaca.

It may be easier to understand, by now, how the meaning of life lies here: this family, this island, and those who live there, are 'his people', the warp and weft of his life in its most deeply rooted aspects, the things he can relate to most immediately and spontaneously. There, he can live fully in the present. It's a very profound definition of wisdom: *carpe diem*. Throughout his wanderings, Odysseus is deprived of that reconciled existence with his world; so he is forced to live, so to speak, in the future and the past alone, feeling nostalgia or hope for Ithaca, never within the present of Ithaca, never in the love and full enjoyment of his island and his family.

It's only when we have again found our natural places in the cosmic order that we can at last live in the present and leave behind the tyranny of nostalgia and hope that was, for the Greeks, the very essence of negativity: for the past no longer exists and the future does not yet exist, they are figures of nothingness – and Odysseus, during the war and then throughout his voyages, is endlessly forced to live in this nothingness, which causes him great suffering. Here we can, between the lines, discern a magnificent doctrine of salvation, of the good life, which locates the meaning of life in harmony with the cosmos, in the love of the present, in what Nietzsche called *amor fati*, the love of what is there.

In token of the power of this wisdom, Odysseus refuses the immortality and eternal youth promised to him by the lovely Calypso if he will stay with her, so certain is he that it is by returning to his place in the cosmic order that he will fully be himself and not by gaining some divine status 'for which he is not made': he prefers a successful life as a mortal to a 'borrowed', 'out-of-place' immortal life that could only be a mistake if not a failure. This episode has an unfathomable profundity: rather than grasping at immortality as if it were a lifeline, it's his life as a mortal and his place in the cosmic order that Odysseus wishes to save. Agreeing to 'save himself' through an immortality that would inevitably remain alien to him would mean betraying and even condemning his own existence, and giving up the place that belongs to him. The great Greek philosophers, especially the Stoics, endlessly reworked this view, developing it, of course, in more explicit conceptual and rational ways, but preserving its most powerful philosophical core.

The theological principle

The *second principle* is more familiar to an audience in the countries imbued by the Christian tradition since it lies at the heart of the message of Jesus Christ, even though – in this respect – his message simply takes up a theme that had long been present in Jewish monotheism: this is the idea that the conditions of the good life are found not in agreement with the cosmic order but in harmony with the divine commandments. Where Odysseus sought his salvation without the help of the gods and often in spite of them in an unceasing effort to get back to his own place in the world by himself, the three great monotheisms offer us salvation, not without God, but with Him: salvation through an Other (God) and through faith.

Religion dominated western thought between the end of the fourth century and the seventeenth century. One consequence for philosophy was that, throughout this period, it lost its autonomy and was reduced to concentrating its efforts on rational analysis and the interpretation of concepts in the service of faith and doctrine which were alone held to be legitimate in the search for salvation. It is curious, be it said in passing, that this fully scholarly, or *scholastic*, view of philosophy is still found, in secularized form, in the French tradition of philosophy teaching in the final year of secondary school: it's as if it were simply a matter, as in the scholastic system of the Middle Ages, of discussing or clarifying notions, the meaning and the hierarchy of the concepts that structure our shared culture.

The religious reply to the question of the good life, in its Christian guise for example, is in my view magnificent. I've given an in-depth analysis of it elsewhere, with the greatest respect, in various books, some of which were co-written with eminent believers. It's just that this reply presupposes that one has faith: for anyone who doesn't, the best thing in my view is, of course, to turn to that secular spirituality known as philosophy.

The humanist principle

The *third great definition* of the 'meaning of life' appeared in the Renaissance, even if, in philosophy, it was Descartes – whose work came later – who symbolized it, since he gave it its own, radically new foundation: this was the humanist revolution, the revolution of subjectivity (the *cogito*, the 'I think', set up as the cornerstone of the whole edifice of modern thought). It extended until the Enlightenment.

How and why could the question of salvation be founded on man, and no longer on the cosmos or on God? This was an arrogance that scandalized the proponents of the 'old' ways: they saw in it nothing but hubris, excess, madness. What, in the view of modern humanism, distinguished man from all other creatures and comprised the source of his irreplaceable value was henceforth his freedom, his ability to 'tear himself away' from natural limits and historical and social definitions: he is not defined by a 'nature' proper to him, not even by a history of which he is the prisoner; rather, he endlessly 'creates himself' by making progress in the sciences and the arts, by the conquest of an ever-wider autonomy, by the endlessly increasing mastery of a sometimes revolutionary history. All of these give him the means to seek out happiness, 'a new idea in Europe' as Saint-Just famously put it.

In this new and fully humanist perspective, the good life is defined no longer as the quest for one's place in the cosmic order, no longer by an immortality won by obeying God, but by taking part in human history. Basically, it is the idea that a man is in some way 'saved', that his life is so to speak 'justified', when he has laid his own brick in the edifice of human progress. In the schools of our childhood, our teachers depicted as heroes in this epic of human genius the 'scientists and builders' who, like Condorcet, Pasteur or Hugo, seemed to embody the best of what freedom, reason and willpower at their highest levels could provide for the advancement of our civilization. It was in relation to the progress of humanity itself, and not in relation to the cosmos or to God, that salvation was now to be measured.

Paradoxically, even though the general viewpoint was now clearly secular, the religious idea of eternity was still not lost – far from it, even though it had changed its 'basic nature' and had, so to speak, become this-worldly. It was entered by a different portal:

you engraved your name 'for eternity' in the stone of the state's buildings and in the libraries of schools, or (in the case of France) in the Pantheon, a name rendered glorious by what it was deemed to symbolize in terms of the inheritance we bequeath to our fellow humans, of progress in knowledge, freedom and happiness. As can be seen, republican humanism, however atheistic, still comprises a doctrine of salvation, a religion of earthly salvation, as people call it. Many people have, with this in view, sacrificed their lives for a political struggle, or even to maintain a scientific idea – proof that they saw in it a meaning that, even beyond death, gave their destinies an eternal dimension.

The principle of deconstruction

The *fourth period* opens with Schopenhauer and blossoms with Nietzsche and Heidegger: this is the period of *deconstruction*, of radical suspicion of all the metaphysical or religious illusions which, at least in the view of the 'deconstructors', lay behind the other principles. They *deconstruct* the idea of a cosmos displaying a harmonious, divine order, and the idea of an all-powerful God (hence Nietzsche's dictum on the 'death of God'). The illusory and deceptive – and *therefore* harmful or even perverse – character of these beliefs is revealed: the problem is that we have subjected our lives to those mirages, instead of living life to the full. When Nietzsche declares that 'God is dead', he adds that this is an unprecedented event, without any equivalent in history, a break that turns the human condition upside down. In the same spirit, Nietzsche's French disciples, such as Michel Foucault, announce the 'death of man', in other words a crisis in the third principle, the *metaphysical illusion* that comprised the humanist conception of a subject who was completely conscious, free and rational, who worked for the progress of humanity and thereby justified his existence. The truth is that this image of the Cartesian subject, transparent to itself and transforming the world through its imperious will, is merely a fiction imposed like an idealist mask on human beings who are in reality multiform, at the mercy of unconscious drives and economic, libidinal, social and cultural processes that crisscross them and endlessly escape their control.

Nietzsche had luminously defined the touchstone of the 'deconstructive' approaches that Paul Ricoeur called the 'philosophies of suspicion' and that Nietzsche classified as forms of 'genealogy': in his view, any ideal that claims to place itself above life impoverishes that life (whether it be a Platonic, religious, humanist or revolutionary ideal), since it reduces life to what it prescribes, to the detriment of all the potentialities it contains within it. But, he adds, life cannot be judged from outside, quite simply because we are in life, immanent to it, and there is no longer any transcendence, either in the cosmos, or in the heavens, or in the history of a progress driven by some vague ideal yet to come.

What appears in the place of this abolished metaphysics? What meaning can be given to life when all the values which, in one way or another, claimed to assign to it a superior value from outside it have been devalued? Nietzsche, without the slightest doubt the greatest thinker of this 'post-humanism' inaugurated by deconstruction, gives a reply which, although it breaks with all previous forms of wisdom, remains – even today – central to our representations of existence. Life, he states, is fully good on two conditions: it must be intense and free, in other words disillusioned. Intensity and emancipation: these are the two essential characteristics that will henceforth claim to define the good life for mortals. We need to gather and harmonize within ourselves the vital forces that will intensify our existences to the highest degree. And they do need to be 'harmonized' since they are in conflict; they mutilate one another and thus weaken us. Here, Nietzsche returns to a theme that was already dear to Spinoza: true joy resides in the intensification of vital forces, and their diminution means sadness. The ultimate criterion that allows us to measure the joy aroused in us by this harmonization of vital forces that gives us the sense of the freedom and intensity of life whose model is found in artistic creation is the fact that we are able to desire to relive, an indefinite number of times, the episodes of the lives we have led. This is the significance of the doctrine of the *eternal return*. This enables us to see that Nietzsche, however much he may have been, in principle, an enemy of any 'doctrine of salvation', nonetheless discovers another link to the eternal that gives, within existence, in immanence to life, a meaning to life, a direction to follow, a wisdom or an ethics – which are quite close, at times, to Spinoza.

Such a profound and paradoxical way of thinking helps us to understand why Nietzsche told his friend Lou Salomé that the truths which he discovered on his mountain peaks, in the frozen solitude of snowy summits, could not be completely expressed, and why they were so difficult to share, given their corrosive, not to say terrifying character.

What we can see today – and this is why I started off with a reference to Stendhal – is that we have entered, for fully philosophical, historical and anthropological reasons, into a *fifth world, a fifth principle supported by a new definition of the good life as the loving life, the life in love.* A good life is a life in which there has been love, whether happy or not, in which love has transfigured everyday life and given meaning to existence. The claim might seem so banal that it demands, of course, to be spelled out.

Why does the 'meaning of life' change from period to period? Is there anything like a 'logic' to this history? How does each new 'principle of meaning' incorporate each time more – and more human – dimensions of existence?

Claude Capelier: Before we embark on that, I think that two points still need to be cleared up, otherwise we won't be able to understand fully the historical succession of the four principles that you've just sketched out or the advent of the fifth.

First, the chronological presentation of the successive forms of wisdom isn't enough: you still need to explain why people moved on from one to the next one. For example, during the Middle Ages, the spread of new technical inventions, the diversification of mercantile relations, trades and social roles led to modes of life for which theology alone was unable to provide an adequate frame of meaning. So philosophers such as Averroes, Maimonides and Thomas Aquinas incorporated a certain number of contributions from ancient philosophy (especially Aristotle's) so as to construct a way of thinking better adapted to the new context. To begin with, they, as it were, philosophically speaking, brought these historical developments under their control; but it later became clear that they had dug a grave for their own theories, since the humanists went on to discover that opening up to new modes of life had much more direct and convincing effects if this new perspective were no longer based on God but on freedom in human beings. Likewise, once the unforeseen effects of the French Revolution had shown up the inadequacies of the rational, moral vision of the Enlightenment, nineteenth-century philosophers broadened this vision so as to encompass the underlying, unconscious dimensions of human life which it had not fully gauged: the historical 'cunning of reason' for Hegel, the class struggle entailed by relations of production for Marx, the will to power for Nietzsche. In short, we need to grasp what, in the evolution of historical conditions and representations, means that one principle of meaning passes over into the next one.

Also, we would be losing sight of one essential aspect of the dynamic process that underlies this 'brief history of meaning' if we didn't emphasize that it expresses a real progress, even though this progress occurs in accordance with unpredictable changes in direction that have neither the coherence nor the dialectical unity postulated by Hegel. This advance from one stage to another combines two complementary movements: first, it gradually opens up dimensions of human life that had hitherto been forgotten, marginalized or repressed (so that each new principle incorporates more of this material than the previous one); second, it moves, so to speak, from the more 'exterior' and 'abstract' (the harmony of the cosmos, God) to the more 'interior' and 'immediate' (our unconscious drives, everyday life, nature within us, love). The essential point is that ever more dimensions are incorporated at the same time. If we look at the first principle, for instance, everything in it which gives human life meaning belongs to the cosmic order, independently of the lives of human beings. Already in the second principle – that of the great monotheistic religions – many more personal dispositions are included: the believer has an individual relation with God. Then, in humanism, it's the possibility of freedom in each person that becomes the basis for the meaning of human life because this is what creates history. Finally, in the phase of deconstruction, potentialities that had been completely left out of the meaning of life are brought into it: sexuality, femininity, childhood and even madness or boredom. If we dig a bit deeper 'under deconstruction' – and this is something you're going to develop – we realize that, underneath these possibilities of human life that are now chaotically liberated, in an 'archipelago' as René Char would have said, there is a common feeling that gives them the coherence they had lacked: everything is grist to the mill of *this* feeling alone, and it alone can 'make sacred' the most varied human features and characteristics. This feeling is love. By giving unity to human experience as a whole, in this broader form, love makes possible a second humanism that doesn't fall prey to the exclusiveness, the limitations and the imperialism of the first.

Luc Ferry: Yes, this history of meaning has a meaning. It goes from the most transcendent (the cosmos) to the most human (love) on a downward scale: a personal God, who is already more human than the cosmos, a free, conscious subject, and then a broken subject whose new dimensions have to be taken into consideration where the rationalist humanism of the Enlightenment had paid it only scant and quite inadequate attention.

Just a quick remark in passing, though it's more than just an anecdote: it's often been said (and it's one of the great arguments advanced by scepticism) that the fact that there are so many different philosophies invalidates philosophy. Since philosophers can defend every kind of thesis, people conclude that philosophy has no credibility. Hegel had already given a very good answer to this objection: he had brought the succession of philosophies within a historical dialectic of the life of the Spirit. We can give a different reply by just saying, quite simply, to make it easier to understand, that the history of philosophy isn't like the history of the sciences: it's much closer to the history of art.

Just as ancient art has never stopped having a powerful impact on us, ancient philosophies still have something to tell us. A person can love romantic art, the art of Ancient Greece and contemporary art all at the same time: they are not incompatible. Likewise, a person can 'live in' philosophies of different periods, however much they may seem to contradict one another. Some of my friends still base their thought mainly on the Ancient Greeks; I know many fine Christian thinkers; several of my acquaintances are great republicans, Kantians who really live in the humanism of the Enlightenment and take this to be the unsurpassable final stage of philosophy. I also have colleagues who are Nietzscheans, or even hardline Heideggereans, close to Derrida, intent on pushing on with the task of deconstructing our – in their view illusory – metaphysical representations.

In short, more than ever these days it is possible to 'live in' the most varied philosophies, at whatever moment of history they may have been conceived, and this is what sometimes gives one the feeling that contemporary philosophy has relapsed into eclecticism. After all, why should anyone prefer the latest theory to be published? Is the last person to have spoken *ipso facto* the one who's right? On the one hand, this new openness to the plurality of interpretations is the expression, albeit unsatisfactory in form (as it can't lead to any coherent synthesis), of our authentic interest in a greater diversity of possible relations to existence; on the other hand, any philosophy that manages to develop in depth a new principle of meaning more suitable to this unprecedented diversity would inevitably, in my view, be superior to the others.

And I think this is possible, if we start out from the following consideration: in this history of the great principles of meaning, in each of the great moments of philosophy that have followed on from one another through the ages, more and more dimensions of the human that had not been taken into account (or at least not sufficiently) in the previous moments have been incorporated. So there is a logic to this history, a gradual humanization of thought, so to speak. This logic is not Hegelian but it goes very deep.

We shall see that, strangely enough, it is connected with the question of death, a question always there in the background, dictating our quest for salvation. These days, we are reluctant to imagine that there might be any progress in history: indeed, we are so critical of Hegelianism and Marxism that this seems impossible. It appears a completely naive idea: 'Oh, come off it – Hegelianism and Marxism are so last century', they keep saying, with the inflexible irony of those who refuse to be taken in by fairy stories or duped by childish fables. I think they are wrong. The idea of progress can be, and probably should be, rethought: it should be conceived of differently from the way those great philosophers of history, Hegel and Marx, imagined it, but in my view it has not lost all meaning – far from it. We simply need to choose another guideline than the one they had followed.

How are we to discover this guideline? In my view, there are three crucial considerations. The first is that, in this history, *we are always moving towards something more human, something that contains more human experience.* New, hitherto neglected dimensions of the human are being taken into consideration in a broader vision than that of previous periods. The second consideration is this: *doctrines of salvation are, if I may say so, increasingly 'efficient', in the sense that they are increasingly credible.* The third point: *our relation to death is changing.* To be saved, in philosophy as in religion, as can clearly be seen throughout the philosophical tradition, from Plato to Schopenhauer by way of Epictetus, Epicurus, Spinoza and even Kant (with his 'what may I hope for?'), is first of all to be saved from death, or at least from the fear of death.

How can these three considerations be brought together? This question opens up exciting but dizzying possibilities. When we consider the first answer, the cosmological answer, we find that the cosmos still takes precedence over a humanity that can find the principle of its destiny only outside itself. In the *Odyssey*, the hero is described as the man who travels from chaos to the cosmos. That is the central idea. The questions that preoccupy us today in human life, whether they are linked to the unique character of the individual, to the irreplaceable singularity revealed by love, to the individual's freedom, to innovative social or political projects, to the education of children or to social equality, are in Homer absent or relegated to the background. The cosmological question is far and away the most important.

If we examine the relation to death that lies behind this doctrine of salvation, we discover that it is based on an idea whose implications the Stoics, as Homer's faithful heirs, tirelessly explored: we are saved from death when we realize that, once we are reconciled with the eternal order of the cosmos, we ourselves become a fragment of eternity. As Epictetus puts it: 'Death is just a passing.' Here we find ourselves in a sort of cosmic mysticism since, at the end of our journeys, we ourselves become fragments of the cosmos and, as such, atoms (so to speak) of eternity. Death is now nothing but the passing from one state to another, from a conscious to an unconscious state, but nothing is lost, nothing is created: we meld with the cosmos and this is another way of responding to our fear of death. Don't be too scared of death, the Stoic is basically saying: it doesn't really exist.

The weakness of this first great 'doctrine of salvation' is that its promise of eternity 'saves' us only in an anonymous form.

When we die, we become a part of the cosmos; we go back to being dust. Not much of a consolation! Of course, Christianity went on to emphasize this weakness, to profit from it, as it were, by trying to offer a more 'tempting' doctrine of salvation.

Claude Capelier: Yes, and the Stoic doctrine of salvation can appear as a consolation only to people who, while still alive, consider themselves to be anonymous links in the chain of an order that transcends them and alone can justify them. In this school of wisdom, death is nothing, agreed, but ... we are nothing, too! It's very striking in Homer: however wonderful, rich and powerful the narrative may be, the characters are merely entities. Even when they are endowed with character traits, they have value only because they are generic, cosmic: they play a role in relation to other character traits in a harmonious system. The only personal trace that a hero can leave in the world is his glory which, of course, turns his name and his story into an archetype of one of the grandiose manifestations of the cosmic order, in which he is, so to speak, completely reabsorbed.

Luc Ferry: The best example of the generic character of mythological characters is the Greek pantheon. As Jean-Pierre Vernant has so clearly shown, the Greek gods are not real persons; they are merely parts of the cosmos. To some degree, when philosophy took over from mythology, it simply transformed what mythology had considered as divine entities into cosmic elements. Ouranos is the sky; Gaia, the earth; Pontos, the rivers; Tartaros, the region under the earth, and so on. They are not characters but parts of the cosmos. This was a world in which the human may indeed have its own place but it's relatively unimportant in comparison with the whole, which is inseparably both cosmic and divine.

In this respect, there is a clear contrast with the Christian conception which replaced the anonymous salvation proposed by the philosophers of the ancient world with personal salvation. The same idea can be found in Islam and Judaism, but it's even more obvious in Christian theology: Jesus is a man and he addresses men. He is the Man-God par excellence. The promise contained in the Gospels, for instance in the episode of the death of Lazarus, is that resurrection isn't just a resurrection of the soul but also a resurrection of the body, a resurrection of the 'complete person', so to speak. Jesus announces that we will meet those we love after death, body and soul. This provokes a theological question that may seem strange: what age will they be; what will they look like? The answer is that they will have 'glorified bodies': we'll meet the people we loved with the loving faces, the eyes, the voice, the smile that we loved. This is no longer a doctrine of anonymous salvation but a personalized and personified resurrection, aware of itself in paradise, in the Kingdom of God.

The third principle, the advent of humanism, went on to lay even greater stress on the value of human experience, 'making sacred' more and more aspects of it. This is finally a vision of the world in which man is at the heart of the system. It's no longer the cosmos, or God, but man who is of greatest significance. This leads to a redoubtable problem: if supreme value lies in the very lives of men, what prospects for eternity, for salvation, can they have, since they are doomed to die? As we have seen, people were forced to 'cobble together' the theory that I really don't like and that Kierkegaard so eloquently mocked: the idea of 'scientists and builders' who add their little bricks to the edifice of progress – this was a way of trying to think up an ersatz form of eternity and salvation that would fit the new emphasis on man as the focus for the question of life's meaning.

Claude Capelier: We might say, if I can sum up, that the 'humanist doctrine of salvation' has one weak point and one strong point. On the one hand, its promise of immortality is, we have to admit, quite 'minimalist': to write one's name in history, inscribe it on monuments, take part in progress by one's creative works or one's deeds remains a pretty abstract and bloodless, even derisory, way of surviving one's death. On the other hand, humanism is incomparably more powerful than the visions of the world that it succeeded since it 'makes sacred' and, in this sense, 'saves' many more dimensions of human life. From a humanist point of view, not only does the potential freedom present in every individual confer an equal dignity on everyone, but there are many reasons for which future generations may be grateful to a person. You might have been a fantastic mother, you might have been a hero who defended your country, or a wonderful poet, or even a hilarious comedian. The diversity of the idea one has of mankind, and of what deserves to survive in people's memories, is here greater than it had ever been.

Luc Ferry: Yes, it's much greater. The reason is that the emphasis is placed on human works, which are extremely varied: you can be recognized and saved almost as much for being a great actor as for being a great resistance fighter, a great poet, a great musician or a great politician. But also as an ordinary citizen who 'did your job', as a mother who's brought up her children, as a school-teacher like the one in Pagnol who was devoted to his pupils or, like Camus's teacher, changed their lives. What is given value, with a view to eternity, is the work – understood as a 'brick in the building' of progress, as a moment of history.

We need to avoid a misunderstanding: it would of course be possible to show that, behind or alongside all developments in thought, in the sphere of meaning and salvation, there lie great scientific, technological, economic, social and political transformations. I'm not out to defend an 'idealist' history of ideas against a materialist history that, like Marx's, requires an analysis of the economic and social processes that contribute to shaping our cultural representations: these things really go together. Actually, I'll later be showing that liberal globalization has intensified the 'deconstruction of traditional values' and indirectly favoured the primacy of love as the basis for couples and families. But if we just stick with the history of ideas for a moment, it's clear that there's a movement towards doctrines of salvation that are both increasingly human and, if I may say so, increasingly 'efficient' – and more efficient because they are more human and thus more credible for us.

In this respect, the following – fourth – period, that of the 'deconstruction' of traditional ideas, values and customs, appears to be a huge intensification of the process whereby hitherto neglected potentialities of the human are humanized and enhanced. On this point, if I were going to rewrite *French Philosophy of the Sixties*, I'd formulate things a bit differently from the way I did when I wrote it in 1985, with Alain Renaut: after all, in one way, the thought of Schopenhauer, Nietzsche, Heidegger and their French epigones could be read not just as an anti-humanism but, at least just as much, as a paradoxical consummation of Enlightenment humanism, that first kind of humanism known as republican humanism.

Claude Capelier: That's right, and Nietzsche often presents himself as a continuer of the Enlightenment – one who, being more consistent than the humanists, takes their own logic to its conclusion and turns it against the Enlightenment itself.

Luc Ferry: Yes, that's the theme that he develops, in the preface to *Daybreak* for example, saying that he is indeed an heir of the Enlightenment, that while Voltaire and the Encyclopaedists stopped halfway, at the stage of critique, he is merely continuing their work of undermining traditional values. What's the result of the operation? Transcendence is eliminated – transcendence as represented by the cosmos, God, the subject, history and progress. Nietzsche and the deconstructors attempt, each in his own way, to develop a doctrine of salvation that's radically immanent to life, to everything 'human, all-too-human' in it, to life *tout court*. A successful life, for Nietzsche, is an intense, free life; it's no longer an aspiration to anything other than life, even if this was just a contribution to 'progress'. And above all, you must live this life without holding back, as there's nothing after it. No beyond, no cosmos, no heaven, no radiant future. You can't put off the question of salvation: it's here and now. Yet again, Nietzsche is close to Spinoza. Salvation is found in immanence, not in transcendence.

Here, of course, we have at one and the same time the means of further diversifying human salvation since we're going to be able to move beyond creative works. It's no longer a question of being a great man (however varied the incarnations of this may be, as we have seen). The twentieth century – which Nietzsche inaugurated, in philosophical terms – went much further in taking into account the many different dimensions of human existence. The deconstruction of metaphysical illusions, of cosmological illusions, of religious illusions, of humanism itself and its mythology of progress made it possible to liberate everything about the human being that had hitherto been hidden under a bushel (this was, for instance, the whole point of modern art). It was a matter of breaking down the limitations inherent in the first form of humanism that was still a humanism of reason and rights, a humanism that reduced the human subject to the question of human rights and rationality. The Enlightenment symbolized this demand, focused as it was, on the one hand, on human rights, democracy and the republic, and, on the other, on reason and science. The age of deconstruction has freed dimensions of existence that went far beyond the juridical and rationalist dimension: as you said, these include the unconscious, the irrational, the animal within us, the femininity of men, the virility of men, everything pertaining to sex and the body, even in the dimensions that the tradition had most disdained. We are witnessing an unprecedented broadening of our vision of human experience, within which intensity and freedom are becoming the two key words.

Modern art, the liberator of the forgotten aspects of existence

The French New Novel (which I dislike, but that's not important here) is a very good example of this spirit of liberation, within narrative, of the non-rational, non-conscious dimensions of inner life. Its forms are adapted to the flow of inner life that obeys not the logic of the plot, nor the logic of chronology, nor the logic of the characters' psychology. The 'stream of consciousness' of someone in a train or in the metro, leaning their head against the window and seeing all sorts of things move by as they travel on, including all sorts of memories too, becomes the object of a narration that no novelist from the 'republican-humanist' tradition would have taken on board. The philosophers of deconstruction (Schopenhauer, Nietzsche and Heidegger, and – in the social sciences – Freud and Marx) put forward new ways of thinking of these newly liberated dimensions of the unconscious and the irrational.

Modern and contemporary art (even though I'm rarely very keen on it for other reasons which we'll come back to) is part of the same process of deconstructing the principles and traditional forms that prevailed in works of art from previous periods. We have witnessed the deconstruction of tonality, of perspective, of narration – in short, of everything aimed at imposing coherence from outside, a coherence that was rational and thus potentially factitious and illusory in the eyes of the deconstructors. Its approach is obviously close to that of the 'philosophers of suspicion'. From this point of view, we could say that these philosophies of deconstruction, which often proclaimed themselves to be anti-humanist (since they deconstructed the first version of humanism, considering it to be still naive and metaphysical) were in a certain sense more humanist than traditional humanism since they strove to lay bare and liberate dimensions of mankind that had been left fallow by the first humanist tradition.

How the great successive principles put forward to give meaning to life have revealed themselves, contrary to a received idea, to be increasingly 'efficient'

So we can see, even if I am here deliberately simplifying matters, that there is a guiding thread through this history of the principles of the good life. The shift from one doctrine of salvation to another is not a random process. These doctrines are increasingly human and more 'efficient' at 'saving' the human as such. There is a guiding thread that moves from greater transcendence to greater immanence, from the less human (the cosmos) to the more human, from the less effective to the more reliable in terms of salvation, from the less satisfying to the more satisfying with regard to the definition of the good life, at least if you don't believe in the great traditional principles (cosmos, God, the man of humanism). From this point of view, indeed, it's much more convincing to reject transcendence and seek a principle of the good life that can work here and now, rather than to try desperately to 'cobble together' a new form of transcendence. To say this doesn't imply any kind of scepticism.

Naturally, it is still possible to live within the traditional visions: as I was saying, I have friends who can recognize themselves in ancient philosophy, in religion, in Enlightenment humanism or in deconstruction; yes, *one can live in philosophies of the past, but we have to acknowledge that they give us an ever more indirect*

and partial access to the contemporary experience of the world.
Clearly, there is still some kind of progress in the answers that the
great philosophies have given to the question of the meaning of
life; they are increasingly human and thus, at least for a humanist,
increasingly satisfying. If you decide that there is something illusory about the old principles, if you think that there is something
correct in the deconstruction of metaphysics (and, personally
speaking, I've never rejected that aspect of the thought of Nietzsche
and Heidegger, and the deconstruction they carry out has always
struck me as legitimate, sometimes even dazzling), you still need
to seek for a new principle able to give an even more correct and
powerful significance to our lives – lives which are themselves
richer and more varied than ever before, but torn between contradictory values and aspirations.

Hence my interest in this fifth aspect of history, love. Love seems
to me to be, at last, an adequate response to what we really think
and experience. Of course, I can perfectly well understand that
for someone who lives in one of the old worlds, and for religious
believers in particular, what I'm saying here may seem debatable
or even sacrilegious. Indeed, this is why I've emphasized the fact
that the old principles still speak to us, and are indeed still 'liveable in'. This is, in my view, more an occasion for dialogue than
for argument – indeed, right now I'm writing a book with Cardinal
Ravasi, one of the most eminent figures in the Vatican: it's a dialogue on the question of the 'court of the gentiles' and discusses
relations between believers and non-believers. This is just to show
that I'm not in the least dogmatic. I'm just saying what I think,
that's all; I'm quite aware that the past worlds were liveable in
and that other people will see things quite differently.

The greatness of European civilization resides in its culture of autonomy

I also think that there's something unique in European civilization,
which consists in the fact that, more than any other civilization,
it is the basis for a project of autonomy, aiming to bring up human
beings to the status of adults and not keep them in that of minors

subject to a cosmological, religious vision, or even to the restrictions of an elitist humanism.

Let me make myself clear: it's not a question of judging civilizations for their good or bad points, like a schoolteacher. Many of them are grand: Chinese civilization, Arab-Moslem civilization, Indian civilization, just to mention a few, have all contributed irreplaceable treasures to mankind. However, European civilization can and must deepen its quest for autonomy: we are living through a time when it is entering what I call the 'second humanism', namely, the humanism of love that isn't simply the humanism of Enlightenment, of progress, of law and of reason. It's a new stage in the conquest of autonomy. Unlike most of my philosophical or intellectual friends, I've always thought that when Francis Fukuyama spoke of the 'end of history', he'd put his finger on something profoundly true. He didn't mean that there wouldn't be any more historical events, which would obviously have been a silly thing to say – history carries on, there are wars, regimes that fall or change; but he realized that the history of this democratic universe (less in the narrowly political sense than in Tocqueville's sense of a civilization of democracy and autonomy) is, on one level, coming to an end, in so far as the human being who wanted to be free has finally achieved self-determination.

In *Was ist Aufklärung?* (*What is Enlightenment?*), Kant says that Enlightenment is the civilization in which the human being finally emerges from his status as a minor, and in this sense an 'end of history' is indeed reached with this civilization of autonomy since we can't imagine any other in which a human being is finally himself, recognized as adult. Things may regress to an earlier stage, of course, and not every continent is part of the same historical trend. The fact remains that the culture of autonomy in every domain (artistic, cultural, philosophical and political) represents something like a definitive moment in human history, a sort of final stage which, so far as we can see today, culminates in this revolution of love that we're going to describe and analyse in the next chapter.

Claude Capelier: So even more than in the first humanism, we should now expect our democracies to be entirely turned towards individuals themselves, towards persons and humanity as such, and not towards transcendent ideals that have been imposed on citizens and that demand them to sacrifice themselves on their behalf ...

Luc Ferry: Yes, and it's precisely here that its difference from the first humanism is clearest. Here again, I wouldn't write *French Philosophy of the Sixties* in quite the same way now: in spite of all its faults and its self-proclaimed anti-humanism, an anti-humanism that we were quite right to denounce, deconstruction will have had, in spite of everything, and often unwittingly or unwillingly, a really positive aspect.

Claude Capelier: I think that these contributions made by modernity were more conscious and deliberate than you suppose. The fact remains that the revolution of love incorporates and moves beyond the contributions both of the first humanism and those of deconstruction. When we met, I objected to the way you underestimated the fruitfulness of the best of the philosophies and works that you classify as part of the deconstructive movement, since in my view I believe they have an emancipatory power and can open up new areas of human life. But I feel that the 'second humanism', as you define it, has the great advantage that it not only brings our points of view closer together – which is of interest only for the two of us – but especially because it puts forward a principle and a philosophy that plug directly into the full richness of contemporary experience.

Luc Ferry: And that's what it aims to do. However, let's not forget that, in spite of everything, in the movement of deconstruction, and indeed in art as much as in philosophy, especially in the second half of the twentieth century, there's not just a real element of virulent anti-humanism but also an element of complete sham – which justified and still in my view justifies the critiques we developed of the sophisms of Derrida, Bourdieu and Foucault. Don't forget that it wasn't just a quarrel over words: when I was a young man, Maoism caused tens of millions of deaths, while some of the most eminent deconstructors and their disciples applauded. The discussions between Foucault and Sartre on the best way of sentencing to death the notary from Bruay-en-Artois – who was innocent, let me remind you – reached the depths of ignominy.[1] In the domain of the contemporary arts, too, concerts of silence and exhibitions without any pictures, piles of rags or lumps of coal placed in a corner and presented as if they were the equal of a Vermeer started to get on my nerves and I haven't in the least bit changed my mind on these subjects. We'll probably be coming back to this.

The fact remains that, at the time when Alain Renaut and I were writing *French Philosophy of the Sixties*, my point of view was still largely that of the first humanism. In plain and simple terms, we were defending the heritage of the Enlightenment against the deconstruction of the Enlightenment. This is what Habermas and Apel did in Germany, or to some extent Rawls in the United States. It wasn't wrong, it was even quite right, in my view, but it still wasn't enough. At that time, I was already looking for what I quite justifiably called a 'non-metaphysical humanism', a humanism that would take into account the objections of the great deconstructors, of Nietzsche and Heidegger: but I hadn't got there yet. I thought that their deconstruction of the illusions of metaphysics was relevant, but I could also see that it threw the baby out with the bathwater – and this is still true, in my view, especially as there was something perfectly legitimate, which I still maintain today, in the Enlightenment ideal, in the ideal of democracy, of human rights, but also in the ideal of rationalism and science. To say, as did Foucault, that 'reason is a form of torture and the subject is its agent' struck me as quite simply stupid and, here too, my mind hasn't changed.

It was only with the man-God that I really started to construct this second, non-metaphysical humanism, that I developed the new point of view of a humanism of love. We'll be coming back to this in the next chapter. I'll be trying to show how this entirely new point of view creates a radically new way of looking at the question of the good life, and how it also totally transforms the situation in the domains of politics, art and education. I'm not going back on what I said in *French Philosophy of the Sixties*, but I *do* think that I've made a great deal of progress, if this word isn't taboo. I now read this history of deconstruction from the

---

[1] This was a notorious murder case in the Pas-de-Calais in 1972: a notary accused of murdering a miner's daughter was seen, by some on the Left, as a typically predatory bourgeois. (Trans. note)

standpoint of what I view as its final stage, that of the revolution of love, and no longer from the previous stage, that of republican humanism. This means that I can complete the critique by adding another, more constructive side.

One can 'live in' old philosophies, but the world can't be understood in any inventive way by sticking to the old principles

Claude Capelier: What you've just said clearly shows that, as you mentioned just now, if one can 'live in' all the philosophical principles, from the most ancient to the most recent, it's impossible to philosophize inventively within the old principles. It's like in art: you can love the art of every period, but nobody's going to keep on building 'Greek-style' temples since this could only be an academic exercise without any inventive aspect. If you want to think freely and creatively, in such a way as to be able to answer questions that haven't been solved yet, you have to work with what comes after the period of deconstruction that is now coming to an end.

Luc Ferry: That's the crucial point. Yes, it's possible to 'live in' the old worlds, very pleasantly sometimes, but the downside is that you can't invent anything in those traditional frameworks. At best, you can apply them to the present time, and this confines us to reading the contemporary world through the eyes of the past. It's feasible, but it generally produces a pessimistic interpretation of the world. Whether we're talking about neo-Thomists, neo-Republicans or neo-Marxists, there's always a fundamentally pessimistic tone at work: 'things are breaking down', 'society's getting more and more selfish', 'the market is invading everything' – in short, 'it's getting worse.' *Laudator temporis acti* – in praise of bygone ages: in short, things were better before. This enables criticism to soar, but it hamstrings the development of any constructive new outlooks. In both these ways, Philippe Muray has gone as far as one can – but what can we get out of it, except for an eternal moralizing-ironic-pessimistic pathos that confers on the person promoting it the appearance of being a genius but, as in *Faust*, a genius or spirit who 'endlessly denies' ('*Ein Geist, der stets verneint*', in Goethe's words)? Yes, pessimism can give rhetorical wings to the words of those who flatter themselves that they haven't been taken in by anything and can thus indulge in a systematic dressing-down of the present age, but this is no guarantee of profundity: for example, there are good reasons for doubting that egotism is any more in evidence today than it was yesterday, that 'people no longer believe in anything' or that our freedoms are any less than in 1950. Read Hugo and Dickens: you'll see whether nineteenth-century society was really better, more just or more cultivated than it is today! And if you go back to the eighteenth century, to the Middle Ages, to ancient times, it's even worse.

Thinkers who live in the past are inevitably prone, however authentic or talented they may be, to turn into managers of a stock of negative judgements. You have your supply of concepts, all nicely polished, which you can apply to the contemporary world, often quite irrelevantly, sometimes effectively, but, either way, they are not of a kind to produce anything new or to broaden people's horizons. For example, in the neo-Republican rhetoric about education, they're always singing the same old song: standards are falling, the market is invading everything and children should go back to wearing grey school uniforms and writing with fountain pens, back to the world of Pagnol and Camus. Every book takes some new object to deplore, wax indignant about and feel let down by, some new reason for lamentation. But even though it happens very often that the criticism is correct, there's nothing we can do about it since it doesn't lead anywhere, except to an impossible step backwards, to restoration: if things have changed, there was some reason for this and you can't grasp the logic of action if you don't take this into account.

1

The Revolution of Love

A New Principle of Meaning

Luc Ferry: After what we've just said, the reader will probably now have a better understanding of the way philosophy is the discovery of great principles of meaning, of the main answers to the question of what a good life is for mortals: a 'discovery' in the proper sense of the word since philosophers do not make any claim to be 'inventing' *ex nihilo*, just from their brains, some self-proclaimed principle supposed to enlighten mankind: rather, they strive to lift the veil, to detect, identify and deploy in a consistent way the as yet unformulated themes on which, in the final analysis, their contemporaries base their views of life. We need to bring to light the meaning and the logic of the vision of the world that now inspires us, to allow everyone to understand it and use it as a guideline.

I've said that we are currently entering, and this is something quite new, a fifth principle of meaning, a fifth answer to the question of the good life, based on the question of love. So, we are in a fifth period of philosophy, that of the second humanism, after the period of deconstruction of the first humanism. However, I haven't yet said either what love was when seen from this angle, as a principle of meaning, or why its flourishing in the sphere of the modern family implied a new reply to the question of the good life. Everyone has some inkling of this, or even a more definite idea, but why, after all, should we start out with this love, this passion as old as humanity? Indeed, even if we accept that there's been a revolution in private life, how can this revolution claim to infiltrate every sphere of existence, including the most public and collective spheres?

How love becomes a new principle of meaning and what kind of love we are talking of. Three reflexive approaches to love: analytical, historical and philosophical

Let's start with the first question: how can we legitimately consider love as a new principle of the meaning of life and thus as a new philosophical principle in this history of the successive conceptions of the good life that I've just described? In contemporary literature, whether we're talking about philosophy, history or the novel, we can distinguish between three approaches to love, even if the third – the one I prefer, the most philosophical of them – is definitely still very far from having been developed as fully as it needs to be.

First, we find attempts to define, by analysing the concepts involved, the different categories or the different names of love, the various components of the way we think of it, to draw from it a set of ideas about what needs to be done if we are to approach an ideal model. Denis de Rougemont was the first to attempt such an analysis – a very exciting one – in his books on the birth of romantic love in the western world. André Comte-Sponville followed in his footsteps with his usual talent, providing the conceptual analysis with a breadth and depth that it had not known beforehand.

Then come the anthropological and historical studies, which aim to describe and interpret the changes that, depending on the period, the social class and the place, have changed our conceptions of love and its role, marginal or central, in the constitution of families. Our writers of the 'history of mentalities', ever since Philippe Ariès, have provided us with some magnificent work in this field: I've already mentioned them and we'll be returning to them in a few moments.

Finally, there's a third, properly philosophical perspective, the one I'd like to explore. While taking the first two approaches into account, it focuses on the way the experience of love renews the question of our relation to the sacred, for instance, how it leads to a making sacred of the other, a transcendence of the beloved, which nonetheless remains completely circumscribed within the sphere of immanence to humanity, a form of sacred even within our 'hearts' yearnings', the most immediate and intimate feelings of human beings. For this is how, in my view, the experience of love becomes, in a period that has deconstructed all traditional values, the foundation for a new form of transcendence, a new way of thinking about the meaning that we give to life.

All of this, of course, needs to be explained, made explicit, and spelled out....

Claude Capelier: Another of love's strengths is that it can potentially enhance every dimension of human experience, since they are all capable of reinforcing it and it has the ability to find, in each dimension, a reason for love. This also sets it apart as the best foundation for values, just when, in the wake of the liberation of hitherto neglected forms of existence, what we seek is to do justice to every possible form of human life, within the limits (of course) of what is democratically acceptable, finally including them within a coherent overall vision.

Luc Ferry: Yes and no. It's complicated, since not every form of diversity is loveable and there are also in the human being many hateful and despicable things. And love never comes without hatred; they are probably two inseparable passions, if only because love leads us to hate those who hurt the people we love, or even, sometimes, to hate those we have loved when they hurt us, leave us, or cheat on us. This history of love, even if it is sublime, even if it reveals a new way of thinking of the good life, is far from being a primrose path. We'll be returning to this when we tackle the third approach to love as a factor in the making sacred of the human. But it is also indispensable to pass through the first two approaches in order to grasp what is necessary and important about them.

The analytical approach or the three names of love: *eros, philia* and *agape*

The first of these approaches springs from what was still in the eighteenth century called *philosophia generalis*, the analysis of general concepts. This analysis may of course have a philosophical dimension, as is the case in Rougemont and, even more, Comte-Sponville, but its first aim is to clarify the notion of love, to spell out the different concepts used to designate it. The two authors I've mentioned – they are favourites of mine – have done exactly this, with considerable talent: Denis de Rougemont, in *Love in the Western World*, for example, and André Comte-Sponville in his fine book, *Ni le sexe ni la mort* (*Neither Sex nor Death*). Denis de Rougemont distinguishes, as does Comte-Sponville (though the latter is considerably more detailed in his philosophical analysis), between three categories or three names of love, drawn from three well-known Greek words: *eros*, *philia* and *agape*. I'll say a few words about them, to make my argument clearer, and because it will be a useful way for me to bring out more distinctly what is specific about the prospects opened up by the 'revolution of love'.

Eros is the love that seizes and consumes. Although it is different in humans and in animals (especially because of what Freud called 'anaclisis' or 'propping'), *eros* remains essentially linked to conquest and sensual enjoyment. But above all, and I am here gladly drawing on the luminous analyses of Comte-Sponville, erotic love, romantic love (especially sexual love) has the particular feature of sometimes deriving more nourishment from absence than from presence. This is the very logic of desire as found already in Lucretius in the *De rerum natura* or in Pascal, in his analysis of *divertissement*: it is part of the contradiction inherent in the libido whereby desire is extinguished as soon as it is sated and is reborn only after a period devoted to other preoccupations and marked by the absence of the object of desire. In this sense, we can say that *eros* is nourished both by the presence of the beloved, when we 'consume' it, and by its absence, since this object has to vanish for a certain time if love is to be reborn.

I'd give a definition of *philia* that's somewhat different from that put forward by Denis de Rougemont and André Comte-Sponville. In translations of Aristotle, the Greek word *philia* is rendered as 'friendship', which is really not very satisfactory since this term does not designate just friendship as such, but also, for example, love for children, which we wouldn't these days identify – or at least not entirely – with mere friendship. What is *philia*?

I'd suggest an image that I find quite an effective way of understanding it: *philia* is the feeling that we have, for instance, when we're out in the street and bump into someone we love but haven't seen for a long while. A smile springs to our lips before any kind of rational calculation: it's a reflex rather than a reflexion. *Philia* is the joy we take in someone else's mere existence. It's joy without reason, so to speak, or at least without any reason other than the existence, the presence, of the beloved. So it's already a form of *gratuitous* love, in the sense that it's free of any calculation. What we have here is a love which, unlike *eros*, essentially takes delight in presence: it's the very presence of the other as such that makes us happy.

The third level of love is the one that Christians put forward first, giving a new breadth to the idea of *agape*. This word, too, has been infelicitously translated by the term 'charity'. These days, we can't stop hearing in this word a sense of pity, which doesn't correspond to the real meaning of the word *agape*. Simone Weil (who was both Jewish and Christian) gave a wonderful analysis of this with reference to the Jewish theory of *tzimtzum*. According to this, the creation of the world wasn't a manifestation of the power of God generating, as it were, an outgrowth of himself, but quite the opposite – the effect of his deliberate withdrawal, with the aim of *letting the other exist*. Like a wave whose ebb makes way for the sand, God withdraws so as to leave room for the universe and for mankind. What Weil attempts to show by connecting *agape* to this theory of *tzimtzum* is the depth of God's love for human beings, its absolutely gratuitous nature: he loves human beings so much that he, as it were, makes himself a 'lack of being so that there may be being'. *Agape* is thus the opposite of *gravity*: it is *grace* itself. Weil sees it as the summit of love, human and divine.

When couples are unhappy, it's often linked to the gravity that weighs them down: we're heavy creatures, and this is because we're always asking for things; we're afraid the other will escape us; we give in to jealousy. Those people who are always asking 'Do you love me?' expose themselves to hearing the reply, 'Of course I love you.' The subtext here is: 'Leave me alone.' When gravity drags a couple down, when one person asks for more than the other, loves more than the other and turns this 'surplus love' into a burden by endlessly requiring that it be reciprocated, this is generally the sign that a split is looming. *Agape* is the intelligence of love, the wisdom of love that consists in leaving room for the other, letting the other be, leaving the other free: this is true love.

In Christian theology, *agape* reaches a very long way: in principle, it goes as far as love of one's enemy. For a very long time, when I was a boy going to catechism classes, I didn't know (and I don't think the priest had much of an idea, either) what on earth this so-called 'love of one's enemy' could mean. I couldn't see how the Jew could love the Nazi who exterminated his family right in front of his eyes; I couldn't understand how you could claim seriously to love the murderer. I saw it (and I think I was largely right) as nothing more than a priest's 'sermonizing', without any real impact on reality.

In the Gospels, however, we find a key to this riddle, in the form of a metaphor that's repeated several times: that of 'little children'. When we love our children, we experience this same *agape*. Not that they are really our 'enemies', of course, but because we love them *whatever they do, even when they misbehave*. This is a model that obviously can't be applied just like that to the bloodiest of tyrants, but it does indicate the nature of a feeling that leads us to continue, in spite of everything, to see the man behind the monster and to treat him humanely even if we resist him.

One of my young readers (Julien Banon – to whom I am most grateful) made a good point to me over the internet: his remark was valuable and I'd like to pass it on to others. He noted that my example of love for children 'even when they misbehave' could, strange as it might seem, apply even to the most dastardly of adults. This at least, he wrote to me, is the underlying message of this sublime extract from the *Notebooks* of Albert Cohen, on Pierre Laval:

> When I'm standing before a brother human being, I look at him and suddenly I know him, I am him, akin to him, his fellow [...]. And because, to some extent, I am the other, I cannot fail to have for him, not indeed the love I have for the people I love, but a tender feeling of complicity and pity.
>
> What is this strange tender pity when I imagine Pierre Laval in his prison? I imagine him, I know him and, strangely, I become him, a poor villain avid for some ephemeral power. Yes, he was a

chief of the *milice*, he served the Nazis, yes, he harmed my Jewish brothers and he scared my mother, and he sent to their deaths children guilty of being born to my people. Yes, at the time when he was powerful and maleficent, he deserved death, a quick death, without suffering. But now he is abandoned by everyone, jeered at, in prison, awaiting sentence. I can imagine him and see him, and suddenly I am him. I can see him in his prison cell, and he is in pain, he is in pain because of the asthma in his chest and, in some peculiar way, in my chest. He is suffering and I can see him vanquished. I can see his crumpled face, his face, the sickly, humiliated face of a man who is doomed and knows it [...]. And I am suddenly pained by the fact that prisoner Laval is in pain, stretched out flat on his belly on the cement of his cell without any chair, stretched out leafing through the dossiers for his trial. He is vanquished, who was once victorious [...], a sad, pitiful cur lying there [...] stretched out writing notes for his defence, in the desperate hope that he won't be killed. And suddenly [...] he knows that he will be killed, he who was once the little boy Pierre, once the victorious minister with his white cravat [...]. Ah, his misfortune sweats on the cement of his cell, and he's all alone in his cell, alone without his wife and without the daughter he loved, alone in his misfortune, and jeered at by all [...]. How can I fail to forgive this wretched man, suddenly so close, suddenly my fellow?

We could say so much about this magnificent text, and give so many other examples of those fallen, wretched tyrants – Ceauçescu, riddled with bullets, still hugging his wife in his arms, the bearded Saddam, filthy, hirsute and covered in dust emerging from the rat hole where he pitifully took refuge. All of a sudden, even when we thought we could finally hate them, and even have the right to hate them, they thrust us into an abyss of ambiguous feelings where pity, and even a sense of brotherhood, strangely well up. It's worth noting, in passing, that it's not just a coincidence if Cohen refers to 'little Pierre', the child in Laval, but also to his own mother, and Laval's wife and daughter, in short, this love which within a family forgives everything, *agape* in its highest form, which can even take the shape of tenderness, pity, indeed, properly speaking, sympathy, *sym-pathos*, 'suffering with' this 'human brother' who is still in spite of everything our enemy. It's a magnificent piece of pleading, be it said, on behalf of forgiveness and thus against the death penalty which makes forgiveness impossible.

At all events, that's what *agape* is, even if it's very difficult: love which even includes love of one's enemy. We have taken another step forward in gratuitousness: it's no longer just love outside of any calculation, as *philia*; it's a love which is, so to speak, 'anti-calculation', almost irrational, anti-rational indeed, at the very least radically anti-utilitarian.

This is what we can learn from this first approach by an 'analysis of the concept of love'. It may take us further, as with Comte-Sponville, to reflecting on what a successful love should be, a love that would reconcile *eros*, *philia* and *agape*, but above all would manage to solve the problem posed by romantic love: if it's true that 'romantic love lasts no more than three years', how can that love be transformed into an enduring union that will live up to the promise of those first torrid years? What Comte-Sponville is basically telling us, with his sense for the right formula, is that we need to move on 'from romantic love [*amour-passion*] to active love [*amour-action*]'. In a similar way, Denis de Rougemont advised us to transform an ephemeral romantic love into a con-structed love, chosen by a firm decision and subsequently devel-oped with the help of intelligence and reason. And this requires more intelligence than passion and involves us sticking to our carefully weighed decision to stay with the same person for our entire lives. If a man fails to do this, he becomes – as Denis de Rougemont puts it so well – a 'Don Juan in slow motion'. In other words, he becomes someone who, every five or ten years, changes partner and embarks on some new passion.

I can see that the project of Rougemont and Comte-Sponville can be legitimate and even very attractive. However, I'm not sure I can follow them all the way: I sometimes have doubts about the real possibility of truly reconciling these three forms of love; I fear that the attempt risks being less a way of moving beyond the intermittent nature of passion and more a mask for the flagging of our feelings. Anyway (and we'll be talking about this on the third level of our discussion of love, that of the phenomenology of transcendence and the making sacred of the other), I think we need to go a little further if we are really going to grasp the expe-rience of love right down to its deepest roots.

Claude Capelier: These analyses are extremely subtle and sugges-tive, but I'm a bit uneasy about the way they seem to want to set out in advance a framework and norms for love which, as someone said, 'has never known of any laws'.[1] It strikes me rather like essays on laughter or the 'rules of art'; the theory very quickly seems to lose sight of the essential: the true nature of its object. Of course, in successful love, as in a fantastic work of art, there's an inextricable mixture of immediate feelings and active reflection. But in these areas, reflection and initiative are valuable only if they prolong desire and feelings. So I think it's a contradiction to propose a 'ready-made' solution to an experience that, by definition, can *only* blow any such solution to pieces. What makes me sceptical is quite simply the way that this type of reflection seems irrelevant to the reality of experience.

Luc Ferry: I do think that the definition of an 'ideal', in love, always more or less comes up against the idea that you need to 'force yourself to live up to it'. The reality is that stories of romantic love (I'm not talking about the love of children, which avoids this fate), like all stories, comes to an end. However, we need to be lucid enough to acknowledge that it's not because a love story comes to an end that it's necessarily a failure, since it might have been a wonderful love story to which we can remain faithful. Obviously, in comparison with the ideal, it may be a failure, but if we use the ideal as a lever to force ourselves to carry on when it's simply over, that won't work either. It's very difficult to be lucid like that. It's like when a CD stops playing: when the Chopin prelude is finished, it's finished. This doesn't mean it wasn't wonderful. Of course, as Nietzsche wrote, *'alle Lust will Ewigkeit'* ('all pleasure desires eternity'): you'd like it to last for ever. If this isn't the case, I don't see how this ideal of 'active love' can really help us. Anyway, from what I've heard, it appears that Denis de Rougemont himself divorced his wife when he fell in love with a woman he was working with. This, at least, is what a person close to him explained to me one day, saying that Rougemont had in his life contradicted the theories that he defended in his thought. I don't know the exact truth of the matter; I never had an opportunity to meet Rougemont, but the anecdote strikes me as both plausible and commonplace.

---

[1] Love *'n'a jamais connu de lois'* – Carmen, in Bizet's opera.

In other terms, I have the greatest respect for this philosophy of love, based on conceptual analysis, but its conclusions seem too ahistorical, too based on a view of things *sub specie aeternitatis*, since they envisage love in its eternal character, whereas it now has a role different from in bygone periods, a role connected with the evolution of the modern family and the modern individual – a development that gives it a new significance in the definition of the good life. It's this new role that particularly interests me, and the second approach, that of the historians, allows us to highlight it more clearly.

The historical approach: how the love marriage replaced the marriage of convenience. The lessons of anthropology and history

In my view, it's absolutely crucial to set out in more detail what I shall be calling a *phenomenology of love*. If I'm here using the term 'phenomenology', it's not for the pleasure of using a bit of philosophical jargon but in order to designate an intellectual approach that seems to me, in every respect, the most suited to the subject since it sets out to 'listen to it', as it were: it provides us with a description in which we look at what really happens, without imposing principles from the outside on it, as was the case in the analyses of the previous concepts, at least to the extent that they concluded by developing a sort of ideal. By 'phenomenology', what is meant here is the description of lived experience, of the phenomenon of love, without any a priori, anything being brought in from outside.

I was saying just now that there were three ways of thinking about love. After a conceptual analysis, the phenomenological approach, which we will now be embarking on, is itself divided into two very different levels: on the one hand, as I said, that of an anthropological and historical 'appraisal', concerned with what, in the course of history, actually happened in the lives of individuals; on the other hand, a properly philosophical description, and not just a historical one, of the immediately given, non-metaphysical transcendence that we experience in love. I'm using some rather rare and difficult words, but I'll make them a bit clearer in a moment with some concrete examples.

Let's begin with the phenomenological, anthropological-historical description of what, on the factual level, happened in the history of human beings in regard to the place assigned by society to love. It's very important, in my view, to keep this in mind since you can't philosophize about just anything or only about concepts, you need to philosophize about reality, too. Philosophy, said Hegel, is 'the understanding of what is'; he also said that it is 'its age grasped in thought' (*'ihre Zeit in Gedanken erfasst'*). This is an excellent definition of the theoretical part of philosophy which justifies us in taking the lessons of history into account.

The great historians of mentalities, such as Ariès, Shorter, Flandrin, Lebrun and Boswell, tell us that, in the Middle Ages, the family based on marriage had absolutely no connection with love, with feeling. Sometimes, of course, as our friend François Lebrun points out with a discreet trace of irony, it sometimes happened that family members loved one another, but this was very unusual and, in any case, it wasn't the aim of the institution. Of course, the Church stressed love and fidelity, but this was also an ideal of general scope that wasn't specific to marriage.

What justified marriage and families in the *Ancien Régime* was essentially lineage, biology and economics. First and foremost, this involved the transmission of one's family inheritance and name to the elder son, and a large number of offspring since you needed a lot of brute strength to manage a farm in the rural, feudal Europe of the time where there was no wage system. The fact that couples didn't love one another, in this context, was obviously not a reason for divorce, as is the case nowadays. Montaigne wrote some definitive things about this topic: I've already quoted them in *The Revolution of Love*, but I'll repeat them here since they shed considerable light on the point of view of his period, even if they shock the anachronistic image we have these days of the 'great humanist' Montaigne. 'Gentlemen,' he basically says, 'never marry your mistress' (*Essays*, Book III, chapter 5). Marrying the woman you love passionately, erotically, is in his view a complete catastrophe: it means, he says, and I'm here quoting his exact words, 'shitting in the basket before putting it on your head'. This eloquent formula shows how, in Montaigne's day, people had the lowest possible opinion of marrying for love. Of course, a man will have a mistress, a woman he loves passionately, but his wife, the person he lives with on a day-to-day basis, is chosen on the basis of quite different criteria, entirely subjected to social reason. It's nice if this association includes a certain tenderness, esteem and friendship, but only on the express understanding that romantic love plays no part in it.

This theme is later found in the middle of the nineteenth century, wonderfully developed in Maupassant's short novella *Jadis* (*Long Ago*). A grandmother, brought up in the principles of the *Ancien Régime*, explains to her granddaughter – who already aspires to making a love match – that marriage and love have nothing in common. The proof, she adds, is that you get married only once, but you fall in love twenty times! She strongly encourages her granddaughter to indulge in affairs. Paradoxically, it's the grandmother who is on the side of dalliance, while the young woman defends what is already a very 'bourgeois' conception of the eternal fidelity of marrying for love.

Not only do people not marry for love in the *Ancien Régime*: they *are married off* rather than *getting married*. This theme is ubiquitous in Elizabethan theatre, the dramas of the Spanish Golden Age and the comedies of Molière. You don't get married; you are married off by your parents, or by the village, witness the custom of the *charivari* which, for this very reason, has aroused so much interest among historians of the family: as it's the village that has married off the young people, it's also the village that reminds them of the law of fidelity. When a husband is deceived by his wife, the unhappy fellow is mounted on an ass, and made to ride through the village under a hail of gibes, gobs of spit and rotten vegetables chucked at his face. Then the husband and wife are settled down in their house and the *charivari* begins. For hour after hour, sometimes for two whole days, people take it in turns to beat against the walls of the house with everything that can make a noise (skillets, saucepans, pickaxes, spades, etc.) to remind them of the law of the community – and it is the community, the village, that is there to remind them. These days, infidelity is a private matter and we observe the greatest discretion when faced with someone who is being cheated on by their partner, but, at that time, it was the other way round: love had, at all costs, to be prevented from disturbing the family and social order as laid down by the common custom. Nowadays, it's love, and even romantic love, which alone provides the foundation for the family; it's the basic cell of a society for which nothing is more sacred than this feeling whose prestige grows in inverse proportion to the decline of all other ideals.

But how did the love marriage ever take over from the marriage of convenience? Edward Shorter puts forward a very illuminating reply in *The Making of the Modern Family*: he sees it as a result of the new category of wage-earners and the labour market brought about by the rise of capitalism. Forced to 'go up to town' to find waged work, individuals escape from the communitarianism of peasant life, and of religion, that reigned in the villages: their wages, however meagre, gave them financial independence and the means of finding accommodation far from the village, and this gave them a new freedom, the like of which women in particular had never previously known.

So marrying for love is a relatively recent European invention made possible by the industrial revolution. Young women, in increasing numbers, had to live, either alone or with a fellow worker, in a small room in the city where they worked and were, for the first time in their lives, paid. Thanks to their wages, they were finally freed of the suffocating supervision of the village and could choose a companion following their own inclinations. They were thus freed from the constraints that still hampered the love lives of middle-class children, like the young people depicted by Molière, forever thwarted by the will of a father who is bent on getting them to marry a partner who suits *his* interests.

Marrying for love therefore first emerged among the working class; the bourgeoisie would take much longer to accept it, for obvious reasons (to do with financial issues and the laws of succession). Only after the Second World War did marrying for love become the norm in every social class, even if it still encountered resistances here and there. As a consequence of this irresistible process, what was looming on the horizon was, of course, homosexual marriage: this springs in a direct line from a movement that aims to disconnect marriage completely from its traditional reasons (biology, lineage, economy) and base it entirely on the same romantic love that Montaigne wanted at all costs to exclude from the family domain.

Over time, love has become – at least in the western world – the sole principle of the family: these days, there is no other. Biology is no longer so important (you can easily love someone without having children with them); nor is lineage (you can fall in love without coming from the same social class, even if, it goes without saying, the weight of social and economic factors won't go away with a simple wave of the wand) – and, for the same reason, it is not constrained by gender (you can perfectly well love a person of the same sex as yourself and desire to marry them). Also, you can be part of a family without being married: you can be a partner in a civil union, or just live together. When I say 'love marriage', what I'm really referring to is the loving family, the family based on love, whether or not it rests on an 'official' marriage, with the two crucial consequences with which I'll conclude this brief anthropological-historical description: the development of a huge love of children, unprecedented in history; and the invention and increasingly commonplace nature of divorce.

As Jean-Louis Flandrin and François Lebrun, in the footsteps of Philippe Ariès, have so magnificently shown, the rise of the love marriage has entailed the birth and progressive intensification of a love of children that had probably never existed in the Middle Ages, though a foreshadowing of it might have been found in Greek and Roman culture; but in any case, it took particular shape, increased in power and conquered the world in completely unprecedented ways. In the Middle Ages, the death of a child was often viewed as less serious than that of a pig or a horse. According to the best historians, for instance Boswell, even at the dawn of the nineteenth century some 30 per cent of children were still abandoned – which was the equivalent of condemning them to death. The story of Tom Thumb is perfectly true (at least, its initial premise is). The emergence and triumph of the marriage for love completely altered this point of view: these days, in the loving family, the death of a child has become the most serious, the most tragic thing that can happen. In my book *The Revolution of Love*, I set out at some length the historical arguments and documents that support and confirm these remarks, and I refer my readers to them for further information (I say this as I know there are many people who still imagine that the love of children is absolutely natural, that it has nothing to do with history, and this is partly true – but very largely false!)

Be this as it may, this exponential growth of love of children within the modern family had major political consequences, to which we'll be returning in the next chapter, with, inter alia, the emergence of a new problematic: that of future generations, in other words the world that we, as adults, will be responsible for leaving to those we love the most: our children.

To stay on the anthropological and historical level a little longer, let's now turn to the second consequence of the love marriage: the invention of divorce. If it's true that romantic love doesn't last, basing marriage on it is building your house on sand. Passion is essentially fragile and variable: that's why increasingly liberal legislations on divorce accompany the rise of the love marriage in the working class. In France, the main date was 1884, the year of the first really substantial law on divorce, in other words the moment when the love match became dominant. But there would be ups and downs.

Indeed, it was these vicissitudes of modern life that Montaigne already had in view in the terrible words of his I quoted a moment ago. His remarks simply mean that he was aware of the fact that basing marriage on love alone, as we do these days, was to risk seeing the traditional family break up in divorce and separation. As I said, 60 per cent of marriages in Europe end in divorce, which of course doesn't mean that the love marriage has failed, but that it's more difficult to live in accordance with love than with tradition. No woman, and no man (of course), would wish to return to the arranged marriage, which proves that the love marriage appears, in spite of its shortcomings, to be an undeniable advance.

These days, the old-style family is often idealized, especially on the political Right – this means the bourgeois family of the period 1850–1950, because divorce was largely forbidden then. Yes, that's true enough, but let's put things more simply: couples loved one another for six days and then bored the socks of each other for sixty years! Men cheated on their wives this way, that way and every way in an institution which people who pander to this nostalgic vision refrain from calling by its name: the brothel. So let's not idealize bygone times for the reason that people didn't get divorced: the traditional bourgeois family no doubt had its qualities, but it was also a family riddled with secrets, lies and infidelities. The women very quickly had to sacrifice their professional lives, and soon their emotional lives too, to husbands who strayed from the marital bed equally rapidly. So it's not an ideal that's as easy to defend as some people imagine. Let's accept, instead, that the life of love may be more difficult these days but still gives us an authenticity, a freedom and an intensity that we wouldn't want to give up for anything in the world.

And this brings us directly to the third approach to love that I mentioned above, the one that describes the dimension of transcendence and the sacred inherent in this feeling given our lived experience of it: we can already see, from a simple historical point of view, how love has become the main principle of what we hold most dear, namely our love lives, our emotional lives and our friendships: at all events, this is the sole founding principle of the modern family.

The philosophical/phenomenological approach to the second humanism, or why love becomes the main foundation of the meaning of our lives

We needed to go through an analysis of concepts and conduct a historical overview in order to understand how our vision of love has changed profoundly, how it has become the principle of what, to our eyes, lies at the heart of the meaning of our lives, starting with our families, our children and our friends. This overview was, however, just a necessary stage before tackling the essential question: why has love become, if not the sole foundation of our values and the meaning of our lives, at least their main component, far more important than the others?

To answer this question, we need to examine *the connections between love, the sacred and meaning*. Let me repeat that I'm not imposing an interpretation from outside, but bringing out, at the very heart of our daily experience, relations that are spontaneously woven between these three dimensions, even among those who haven't become aware of the fact. It is this non-metaphysical description of human realities that is called *phenomenology*.

First of all: what is the sacred? Contrary to what common opinion supposes, it's not simply the opposite of the profane; it's not the religious or not, at least, the essential element of the religious. The sacred, as its name suggests, is that for which we are ready to sacrifice ourselves. Values are sacred when I could ultimately die for them (rightly or wrongly, that's not the issue); sacred is that for which I would be prepared to risk my life and even, if necessary, give it. Now in Europe we've witnessed an unprecedented deconstruction of the traditional figures of the sacred (we'll be coming back to this when we discuss political and artistic questions). As a first approximation, one could say that, in the history of the relations between Europe and the sacred, people have died en masse (in wars, massacres, revolutions) mainly for three 'causes': for God, for their country or for the revolution. These are the three great figures of the sacred in the history of Europe.

There have been wars of religion, nationalist wars that have created tens of millions of dead and equally murderous revolutions. Today, the three great figures of the sacred are practically dead among the younger generation, at least in this old Europe of ours (elsewhere, alas, things are rather different): this is one of the most profound effects of the formidable 'deconstruction' of traditional values that characterized the European twentieth century in every area. Generally speaking, at least in Europe (and this history is European first and foremost), nobody is ready to die for God, for their country or for the revolution. Of course, one can still find religious believers, patriots and even a few revolutionaries. However, none of them still has a really sacrificial relation to their ideal, even less a relation for which they are prepared to kill or die.

On the other hand, a phenomenology of the contemporary sacred would clearly bring out the way that *the only people for whom we would be ready to die, to risk our lives, perhaps even to lay them down, are the people we have made sacred by love. Love produces, in regard to those we love, an effect of making sacred.* This is what marks a transmutation in what founds the conception of the meaning of life in Europe today. Only on behalf of human beings are we now prepared to die, and not for abstract entities: neither God, nor country, nor revolution. And these people are not just our nearest and dearest, those whom we love most directly. They all represent – as the whole history of the emergence of secular humanism suggests – our neighbour, not just someone to whom we 'feel' close but quite the opposite: the anonymous person, the one we know only at a distance, one who, as a result of our fellow-feeling, by a kind of capillary action, ceases to leave us completely indifferent. I wouldn't say that we're ready to die for such a person, but, yet again, his fate arouses our interest, indignation and sometimes our active intervention, witness the various humanitarian actions that have become increasingly common over the last forty or so years.

We must avoid the simplistic conclusion, so empty and facile that it becomes wearisome, which consists in deducing immediately from what I've just said that the revolution of love leads only to a retreat into the private sphere. As if, after the waning of the great causes and the utopian dreams, only the family was left. As we shall see, it's completely the opposite. *The truth is that this history of private life, quite contrary to the commonplace prejudice, leads to a more open, diverse and active sense of fellow-feeling for the other than at any other period. We can always decide – but in the name of what golden age? – that this is not enough, that our societies are not intervening actively enough on behalf of the poor, the wretched, the victims of massacres. But when or where has any society done so more than ours? In fact, the revolution of love changes our practices and our collective ideals at least as much, if not more, than our private behaviour.*

Our political projects, now guided by a preoccupation with future generations; our concern for the weaker members of society; our increasing awareness of the risk facing the planet: all these are an expression, in collective life, of the change in perspective brought about by the revolution of love. Our societies are said – yet again by those who don't take a moment to think about it or even glance at history – to be more 'individualistic', more selfish and greedy than ever. But objectively, since this is not just a matter of personal opinion, it's completely the opposite that's historically and factually true: never has our concern for the other been as great as it is these days, and it's not just empty words. We're forever being told that the world of money, banking and markets has ended up dragging us down to hell, to the 'economic horror' where greed, speculation and unbridled competition alone make the rules. Globalization, far from being a happy state of affairs, has – it is claimed – merely made the poor poorer and the rich richer, in contempt of any ethical consideration.

Of course, not everything in these complaints is false. As Pascal emphasized, generally speaking, no shared opinion is entirely false. Admittedly, certain forms of inequality have become more pronounced, but on what objective data is based the idea that moral decline is a definite fact? At the risk of appearing naive, I have to say that I think the complete opposite is true, at least in this old Europe of ours. This is not an ideological judgement of mine: if you consider the facts and don't just stay on the level of subjective impressions, the discourse of decline just doesn't stand up. You have only to ask it exactly what ideal past it has in mind and it starts to look uncertain. Where did it get the notion that 'things were better before' or somewhere else? In what century? In what country?

This is where the pessimists get fazed and their arguments hazy: they have the greatest difficulty in coming up with some historical or geographical point of reference that will support their claim. It's easy to criticize the flaws of the present, the inequalities, the economic crisis: but it's considerably more difficult to venture any clam that there was once a golden age. All the work done by historians, let alone everything we read in literature, show clearly that the olden days were in every way harsher and less concerned about the other than are our welfare societies, which are, in the final analysis, more gentle and benevolent than every other form of social and political society known hitherto. Whatever people may say, our democracies provide unprecedented spaces of freedom, as well as a permanent concern for the other that, far from being merely a matter of words, is constantly being translated into deeds. Read Hugo and Dickens on the nineteenth century, Voltaire on *lettres de cachet* in the eighteenth, Hugo (again) on the Middle Ages or Tacitus on the Roman Empire and you'll see how wretched were the lives of ordinary people, how selfish the mighty, how self-absorbed ('every man for himself') the destitute, how cruel the tortures and executions, how abandoned the sick, the handicapped and the unemployed and how violent the large-scale banditry and the savage hordes.

Look at the rise in humanitarian action. In France as in other countries, it is a particularly clear example of the shift from love of one's nearest and dearest to love of one's neighbour. One day, when I'd been giving a lecture on humanitarian action to Robert Badinter and his friends in the Académie des cultures, he made one of his customary brilliant remarks: 'The fundamental formula of humanitarianism,' he said, 'is basically just a variation on the canonical formulation "do not do unto others what you would not wish to be done to you", namely: "do not let be done to others what you would not wish to be done to you."' This 'do not let it be done' expresses the struggle against indifference, and this is what characterizes modern humanitarianism and is directly connected to the revolution of love, to the rise of the modern family within our European societies. This sense of fellow-feeling that we cannot stop ourselves from experiencing for the other, however fleetingly – this feeling that his fate cannot leave us completely indifferent, even when we don't know him, the idea, at any event, that we cannot be untouched by the tragedies that strike down other peoples, however different their way of life may be from ours – is simply a direct consequence of the fact that this feeling has grown in our private lives.

Let's remember the not-so-distant time when people were stonily indifferent to massacres in the colonies, to the segregation or exploitation that affected whole populations, to child labour in faraway countries and even to the most appalling genocides. We find it hard to understand how we let the Jews be exterminated without bombing the death camps, right up until the end of the Second World War, with the excuse that we needed to concentrate on war and resistance. The genocide of the Armenians by the Turks, that of the Libyans by Mussolini's troops, left public opinion in a state of complete indifference at the time. We worry about these things now, but nobody did then. Of course, I'm not naive; I know perfectly well that selfishness hasn't disappeared, or violence and injustice: who would be short-sighted or cynical enough to claim the contrary? And the evident fact of progress doesn't mean that we can resign ourselves to the misfortunes and inequalities from which so many men, women and children suffer: of course, we need to do our utmost to improve their lot. Nonetheless, one would also need to be blind not to see that we feel for suffering populations and act on their behalf more than ever, whatever the limits of our intervention. This is extra evidence that the revolution of love, far from being a private affair, has already had a far from negligible influence on the public sphere.

Claude Capelier: Love gives value to, and indeed makes sacred, whole dimensions of human life, individual characters of every sort: we are susceptible to the charm of the men and women we love; we find their originality, their characteristics, even their little quirks and foibles, 'brilliant'. When love becomes the sole or at any rate the main fundamental value of contemporary civilization, this openness to the diversity of human expressions, which is one of its main tendencies, inevitably entails an additional sensitivity to the most different people, populations and problems. The range of things that can potentially be made sacred in the name of love is far greater than was the case for the four previous principles of meaning. This is why, far from enclosing us in the sphere of intimacy, love impels us to intervene in the public sphere.

Luc Ferry: One of the celebrated formulas of love – 'That's just what I love about you! [*ça, c'est tout toi!*]' – clearly brings out the way we pay homage to singularity. In a magnificent and celebrated passage in his *Pensées*, Pascal asks what it is that we love in the other. Is it his qualities that we love? But people can accidentally lose their qualities. They can lose their beauty and even their intelligence: will our love for them vanish as a result? Of course, we love the intelligence, beauty and charm that can trigger love and even maintain it, but, when we really love a person, what we love is quite simply that person, and that's why we can continue to love them even if some accident deprives them of their 'qualities' – so long, of course, as the person in question is still the same person. That's the meaning of the celebrated 'Because it was him, because it was me' that Montaigne said about La Boétie. When we say to someone 'That's just what I love about you', what we're referring to is an absolute singularity, one that is, in the true sense of the word, irreplaceable: this is what we find loveable.

If we extend the parallel you were suggesting between personal love and the political effects of the revolution of love, we need to acknowledge that the first humanism, even in Kant (who expresses it in the grandest manner), considerably underestimates the dimension of fellow-feeling. When we see images of an Iraqi or African father weeping over his child who has been killed in the war, we tell ourselves – unless we're brutes or beasts – that he has the same feelings we would have in his place. Even if we don't know him, even if he doesn't have the same language, the same religion, the same skin colour, we know he feels the same suffering when faced with the death of the person he loves, and we cannot remain completely indifferent. What I'm saying is this: it is not out of 'respect', i.e., on the basis of the application of the Kantian categorical imperative, that we fight against indifference ('act according to that maxim whereby you can, at the same time, will that it should become a universal law'). It's not some rationalism of respect but a respect motivated by the fellow-feeling ultimately rooted in the feelings that emerged within the modern family.

So it's absurd to see the revolution of love as a mere retreat into private life. This reaction is simply a sign that people are still caught up in the traditional categories of liberalism or socialism. These are, as I suggested earlier, systems in which private life is on principle excluded from the public world: but this is a great mistake. We'll be returning to this in the chapter on politics where we'll see that the revolution of love transforms relations between the private sphere and the public sphere, especially with the emergence of our new preoccupation with the fate of future generations.

From love as a form of making sacred to love as a bearer of meaning

So far, I've been attempting to explain the connection between love and the sacred, but I haven't yet said anything about the connection between love and meaning. So let's turn to this phenomenology of love as a new principle of meaning. As an Arabic proverb puts it: 'A man who has never in his life come across some reason for losing his life is a poor man, since he hasn't found the meaning of his life.' This fine, simple adage aims to show how interwoven are our relations with the sacred and our relations with meaning. Even if we have lost sight of the fact, it's easy to realize, if we think about it just for a moment, that *the values for which we would be prepared to lose our lives are obviously those which (secretly, but permanently, and in every area of our lives) give meaning to our lives or create meaning in our lives.*

As regards the indissoluble link between the sacred and meaning, we need to ask what the replacement of the previous principles of meaning by love entails for our conception of the sacred and our idea of what a 'good life' should be like. In fact, we are no longer just in a humanism of rights and reason but in a humanism – what I call 'second humanism' – which, unlike the first, is fully open to 'otherness', to the diversity of civilizations and which, more generally, cultivates, promotes and enhances a much wider range of the dimensions of existence in which human beings can, as the saying goes, 'realize themselves'. It is of some significance that Europe has moved from the colonial imperialism of a Jules Ferry, the real symbol of the first republican humanism, to public assistance for development, which clearly illustrates the demands of second humanism.[2]

Let's take this further. I've already mentioned my own project of developing a 'non-metaphysical humanism', a humanism which, unlike the first, is not vulnerable to the attacks of Niezschean–Heideggerean deconstruction. Now from this point of view, it is quite remarkable that this principle of love, seen from the angle of a phenomenology of lived experience, is not a metaphysical experience; it is not vulnerable to the 'deconstruction' of traditional humanism as carried out by Nietzsche and Heidegger. Why? I don't want to get into an over-sophisticated argument here, so let's just say that this transcendence of the other that I experience in love is not some abstract principle or idealist illusion, a value that has come down from a cosmic or divine heaven, but a lived experience – indeed, the most immanent and spontaneous experience there is: love, like beauty, grasps us as a sort of transcendence, and yet this transcendence, which can at times make me 'come out of myself', from my egocentricity, is most directly demonstrated in the most secret intimacy, in the most radical immanence to my subjective awareness. We do experience the transcendence of the other, of his otherness, but this transcendence does not come down from on high, from the cosmos or from God, or even from practical reason and the simple 'respect' that is rationally owed to others. This transcendence is experienced nowhere else – to use the cardinal formula of Husserl's phenomenology – than in the most intimate immanence there is, the one expressed in every language by the universal metaphor of the 'heart'.

The first – republican – humanism had borne the full brunt of the 'hammer blows' (Nietzsche) of the philosophies of deconstruction. They denounced – often erroneously but sometimes with powerful arguments – the arbitrary limitations and partly illusory nature of its presuppositions. But the second humanism is not affected by the habitual objections of 'deconstruction', being born from the experience of a transcendence that is no longer, properly speaking, 'metaphysical', a transcendence that grasps us in what Husserl calls the 'lived world' (*Erlebnis*) without needing to go through some entity that is supposed to 'stand over and above'

---

[2] Jules Ferry (1832–1893) was a prime minister of France in the Third Republic: he was a defender of secularization and colonialism.

life, in short, without yielding to the traditional illusions of metaphysics.

Claude Capelier: It seems to me that there is a close relation between the 'liberation', as we have called it, of the hitherto neglected dimensions of existence under the impact of 'deconstruction' and the emergence of love as a new foundation for the values that are most precious to us these days. The artists who have opened up new paths where their predecessors had merely seen dead ends, the philosophers who tried to think through strata of existence that had so far remained unthought, the individuals who have thrown off the weight of conventions, have all, so to speak, turned something that had long been rejected into something loveable or attractive. So the only point in common to these approaches, which follow the most varied paths, is love. I conclude that the revolution of love marks a deeper level in the period of deconstruction: if we dig deeply enough beneath the debris left by deconstruction, we will find the principle of open coherence provided by the revolution of love.

Luc Ferry: Yes and no. Perhaps we need to specify in more detail the relations between the second humanism and the previous two stages of the 'brief history of meaning' that I sketched out above. We'll be discussing them in greater depth and more explicitly in the next chapter, but let's say straight away, to avoid any misunderstanding, that what I call the second humanism makes no claim, as did Heideggerean deconstruction for example, to abolish the first. Reason and human rights are still cardinal values, and I do not reject the Enlightenment, I do not see it as just one of the illusions of the 'metaphysics of subjectivity' (Heidegger), of 'nihilism' (Nietzsche) or of 'bourgeois ideology' (Marx).

In my view, we need rather to reinterpret it in the light of a principle that I take to be superior. Deconstruction led to a radical anti-humanism (the 'death of man' in Foucault) which I continue to reject. However, the deconstruction of traditional modes of life really did liberate the dimensions of human being that we mentioned just now: the unconscious, the body, sex, the irrational, and so on that traditional forms of life relegated to the background or even fought against as 'impure'. Indeed, whether in the great religions or in the great rationalist metaphysical systems and up until

the first humanism, what was seen as important was always per-
spicuous rationality, the beauty of form, the intelligible rather than
the sensible, the idea rather than the flesh, coherence rather than
madness, order rather than the festival, and so on. In short, what
was valued was Nietzsche's 'Apollonian' rather than the mad,
'Dionysian' aspects of existence. People happily marginalized the
dimensions of life that I've just mentioned, let's say the 'irrational'
or 'disorderly' dimensions of the person, the dimensions that were
foreign to what Platonic or Cartesian reason highlighted. Not only
were they not liberated but they were, in the school system of the
French Republic, for example, permanently suppressed. Uniforms
were the symbol of this: nothing was allowed to overstep the
mark.

In contrast with the traditional family, the love marriage is a
marriage chosen out of passion, and thus it gives a central place
to erotic love – which was barely tolerated in the family in previous periods. One objection that will be raised here is that love
has always been seen positively in Christianity and that it was
predominant in this old Europe of ours. Even in my childhood,
85 per cent of French people declared themselves to be Catholic.
This is doubtless true, but while the Church has always prea-
ched love, everyone knows that it has never given value to erotic
love, let alone romantic love – which, indeed, it has always
been critical of, seeing it as running the risk of a dangerous pas-
sivity and even of forgetting the only love of any value, love 'in'
God, as Saint Augustine put it. What is emphasized in Christian
ethics (as in republican ethics) is courage, valour, the victory over
sloth, over the animal aspect in us, over the body, over sex, and
so on. Tenderness and brotherhood are good, but romantic
love is not.

By setting passion and eroticism at the heart of marriage, and
allowing the wolf to enter the sheepfold of the family, as it were,
people have foregrounded a human (no doubt, in the Church's
eyes, all-too-human) feeling. The fifth principle (love) is, in this
regard, at least partly, an heir of the fourth (deconstruction), even
if it is a paradoxical heir since it questions the deconstruction of
humanism at which the fourth principle simply, and wrongly,
halted: hence the necessity for what I call a non-metaphysical
humanism. What we have here is a real *Aufhebung* (a 'moving
beyond while preserving') in the Hegelian sense, and this is what

I will retain from Hegel's philosophy of history. Although this succession of five principles doesn't form a rational system, there is still a logic of history at work in it, there is still progress (and, if we are humanists, we can see it only as progress). And this naturally needs us to tackle the question of the changes that the revolution of love produces in the political sphere.

How the revolution of love is destined radically to transform collective issues and political life

As I have said, philosophy was a doctrine of salvation without God, a quest for the meaning of life just by the 'means available' to humans, without any claim to immortality, by the lucidity of reason alone. It proposes a *secular spirituality*. Love, which by definition is potentially applicable to all our dispositions, allows each of our activities to be attached to a principle of meaning of unparalleled power within a coherent philosophical *system*. The *secular spirituality* that we shall be describing in the following chapters should be understood in the sense in which Hegel spoke of a philosophy of Spirit: it rests on the idea that human activities, including the most material, are always enfolded within a spiritual problematic, under the gaze of Spirit, of intelligence, which changes the situation. This is the mark of humanity. Freud clearly showed that, even in the most apparently animal act of love, we are actually 'propping' something on the sexual act of reproduction properly speaking – and what we are 'propping' on it is countless 'preliminaries', meaningful expressions, 'spiritual' words and gestures that accompany desire and pleasure, during and after intercourse.

We can probably find (as do certain biologists specialized in ethology) animal equivalents for all our practices, whether in education, art, economy, politics or law, but what characterizes the spheres of human activity is the fact that they are all included within spiritual or intellectual activities, a vision of the world based on a philosophical point of view. This, schematically speaking, is what Hegel calls the 'life of the Spirit', and this is where I will go along with him, even though I don't share the ideally systematic view of his philosophy of history. What I'd like to show is how greatly the revolution of love affects the three spheres of the life of Spirit that strike me as crucial and go beyond the limits of private life: politics, education and art.

Education is carried in the family but is also extended in teaching, at school, in what in French is called '*l'Éducation nationale*' or, in the language of the first humanism, '*l'instruction publique*'. Art relates to an intimate experience, of course, and taste, as the adage has it, is 'subjective', but it is also one of the places of common sense or common meaning around which humans gather, crossing national frontiers and social classes: for that reason, art can produce what is called 'great works'. The concertos of Mozart are played in Beijing as well as in Bombay or London. And finally, I don't need to explain that *politics* is the public sphere par excellence.

It is really exciting to see how a revolution that initially seemed a private matter can in a democracy profoundly reshape these three spheres. I say 'in a democracy' since it is the essence of a democracy to reflect the most fundamental preoccupations of individuals even in political life, to be, more than any other regime, receptive to their influence.

2

Politics at the Dawn of a New Era

From the Revolution of Love to Care
for the Fate of Future Generations

Luc Ferry: The triumph of the love marriage via the birth of the modern individual emancipated from traditions, but also via the deconstruction of traditional values that liberated hitherto more or less concealed dimensions of human life, gives birth – we have just seen why and how – to a new vision of the world, an unprecedented conception of what really gives meaning to our lives. For an ever increasing number of individuals, friendship and love, especially towards our children, but not exclusively, are gradually becoming a new principle that can lay the foundation for our vision of existence and the spiritual values by which we understand our history and our most decisive choices.

Even if this revolution of love was first made manifest in private life, we need to realize that it is also the key to a comparable overhaul in the public sphere, including – perhaps above all – an area from which intimate passions are deemed to be excluded in favour of interests alone: politics. This is why I would now like to show how the revolution of love leads to a profound reconfiguration in our political ideals and practices – a process which will inevitably soon change the face of our democracies. Once we have set out the paths by which this new principle of meaning may become embodied in the component of our collective life that appears furthest removed from it, we will be able to grasp its no less spectacular influence in the field of art and of education.

The irresistible decline of the two great centres of meaning on which politic has been focused fui iwu centuries: the nation and the revolution

Let's cut to the chase: ever since the French Revolution, two great centres of meaning have organized European political life: the nation and the revolution. I use the word 'focus' to suggest something analogous to the vanishing point in a perspective painting, the point from which every particular aspect of the representation is organized, finds its just proportions and gains its full meaning. The two political principles I have mentioned have played a quite analogous role: they gave an overall significance to all the particular plans – economic, social, educational, cultural, and so on – which ministers were there to promote in different governments. On the Right, the emphasis was laid on the national or patriotic idea; on the Left, the revolutionary idea. There were, of course, possible overlaps between the two: the revolutionary ideal could be imbued with nationalism or patriotism. The fact remains that both sides preserved their own system of values and of interpretations, whose logic excluded those of the other side. When I was young, the Gaullist newspaper was called *La Nation* and all my friends, in May 1968, whether they were Trotskyists, Maoists, libertarians or Communists, inevitably were or called themselves 'revolutionaries'. There were, as they say, great plans afoot, for utopia on the Left and even to some extent on the Right where 'a certain idea of France', embodied in General de Gaulle, represented in the eyes of his supporters an ideal of grandeur superior to particular interests and to party political quarrels. It was a sign of the times that, when General de Gaulle died, several newspapers used the same headline: 'France is widowed.' Without wishing to be cruel, for which politician these days, of whatever party, could a newspaper in the same circumstances use a similar headline without appearing absurd, completely ridiculous?

The reason is, of course, that as a result of the great deconstruction of traditional values I have already discussed, the two 'focuses' of meaning in question – the nation and the revolution – are now, for the younger generations and even for ours, if not quite dead, at least terribly stale, like a glass of champagne that's gone flat and lost all its fizz. Of course, and we referred to this in the previous chapter, there is, and will no doubt long remain, a handful of extreme nationalists, of old-style patriots, just as there will always be a few revolutionaries. Democracy is essentially the place where all counter-cultures can exist – and this is why they can never entirely vanish. This is more a pose, however, than real combat, more a posture than a realistic vision of the world, and nobody seriously believes that the leaders of these extremist movements will one day be able to wield power. Furthermore, those who still, in West Europe, claim to be hardline nationalists or to be seeking revolutionary utopias endeavour to gather the support of their fellow citizens at the polls, not to impose their programmes by violence, which represents a major difference from the Maoist language of the 1960s which appealed to mass violence to hang, as the time-hallowed expression put it, 'the last boss with the guts of the last priest'.

Contrary to the received idea, the twilight of traditional ideals does not announce the 'disenchantment of the world', the 'age of emptiness' or 'democratic melancholia', but quite the opposite: the 're-enchantment of the world'

Does the death agony of the 'great schemes' of the nationalists and revolutionists announce the 'disenchantment of the world', to repeat the title – itself a homage to Max Weber – that Marcel Gauchet gave to one of his best books? Are we about to embark on the 'age of emptiness', as Gilles Lipovetsky suggests? Are we doomed to 'democratic melancholia', in Pascal Bruckner's words?[1] Basically, these three formulas express similar ideas both on the level of the diagnosis (the end of utopias and the end of great

---

[1] Ferry is referring to three recent books: Gauchet's *Le Désenchantement du monde*, translated as *The Disenchantment of the World: A Political History of Religion*; *L'Ere du vide* by Lipovetsky, on contemporary individualism; and Bruckner's *La Mélancolie démocratique*, on the continuing need for active citizenship in an age of widespread 'melancholia'.

passions) and of prognosis (the advent of a period lacking any enduring convictions or exciting collective plans, torn between excessive but ephemeral crazes and a vaguely depressive sceptical individualism). Is this really what lies in store for us?

In my view, not at all. There is an undeniable moment of truth in these expressions, and the three books I've mentioned bring this out brilliantly. What we are living through is not the end of the sacred or of meaning in politics; quite the contrary, it's the emergence of a new figure of the sacred, what I call 'the sacred with a human face', in other words the making sacred of the other, linked to the emergence of a quite new collective problematic, to some extent based on the model of the love marriage – one that will find *ever greater expression in an unprecedented concern for the welfare of future generations.* This is a sort of refraction of private life into public life. It establishes a concern for generations to come as a new focus of meaning whose role will gradually become, in the next few years, analogous to that played by nationalist or revolutionary ideas.

What world are we going to leave to those we love the most, our children and, more generally, the young, those who come after us? This, it seems to me, is the new political question, in fact the only new one to have arisen for two centuries, witness the fact that the ecological movement – which was the first to realize this – is, if you think about it, also the only new political movement since the French Revolution. Far from being a coincidence, this is a direct consequence of the rise of a concern for one's children, a concern that itself is produced by the revolution represented by marrying for love. Concern for future generations opens up a shared space between the private sphere (the feeling that flourishes in the family and leads us to make sacred those whom it literally transfigures) and the public sphere (the future of young people and, beyond them, of humanity as a whole). There are at least two reasons for this. First, the world that we're going to leave to our children is by definition also the world we are going to leave to all humans; second, by choosing political trends for all people that we deem to be the best possible for our own children, we are starting out from a criterion that is a reliable enough basis for us to seek the fairest, most generous and most sensible solutions. To put it more simply, when I was minister of education, the reform I introduced was not just on behalf of my three daughters. It was, self-evidently, a reform on behalf of all the children of France. It was a collective measure, not just something meant for private life. However, I never stopped asking myself this question which, I think, constitutes the best criterion: if this reform were to be applied to the young people I love the most – my daughters – would I still introduce it? Would it really be this reform that I'd introduce?

Ecology is the first new political movement that can compete with the age-old domination of liberalism and socialism

I'll dwell on this for a moment longer since it's an essential and quite uncontroversial point: it's no coincidence that ecology is the sole new political movement since the French Revolution. Liberalism and socialism have dominated our political representations since the start of the nineteenth century, under the crossfire of criticism from the counter-revolutionary extreme Right and the extreme Left of the anarchists, or the followers of Hébert or Babeuf. In other terms, the political landscape was already completely filled in the immediate wake of 1789. If, these days, ecology can threaten the monopoly that was long enjoyed by these doctrines, this is precisely because it's the only movement that, apart from its various failings, at least has the merit of raising the question of future generations, thus re-establishing what are probably the most fundamental elements of any grand politics worthy of the name. First, a long-term problematic in a society where short-termism has become a real bane in politics, in finance or the media. And second, a sacrificial dimension, so to speak, in the sense that we need to make considerable efforts to preserve the chances of a good life in the future for the people we love.

Ecology – and this is its main strength – thus brings into the heart of the political debate the question of the future and the various sacrifices required from us by our duty to leave to future generations a world in which they can flourish. It allows us to move away from the 'short-termism' that comes with globalized capitalism and democracies ruled by public opinion.

The 'second humanism' will reorganize all the big political questions under the purview of this new focus of meaning, namely, the question of future generations

The central role that concern for future generations, in the wake of the birth of the modern family, will thus be playing in our conception of politics does not lead solely to paying more attention to the problematic of the environment: far from it. It also places at the heart of our preoccupations the imperative of reducing public debt (are we going to impose the burden it represents on our children?), the necessity of avoiding a 'clash of civilizations' (are we going to leave to our young people a world at war with populations in the grip of fundamentalism?) but also the question of the future of social welfare in the process of economic and monetary 'dumping' comprised by globalization today (will our young people still be able to pay for their retirement and finance unemployment benefit, health insurance, etc.?).

In other words – and this is the essential point – it's *all the big political questions, not just the questions related to private life, that will be reorganized under the purview of this new focus of meaning comprised by the problematic of future generations, a problematic that gives depth to the future and support to the idea of indispensable sacrifices.* This is no longer the case for those other focuses of meaning, now abstract and faded, and indeed purely verbal: the nation and the revolution.

This complete reorientation of politics around the question of future generations is the expression, in the public sphere, of what I call the 'second humanism'. And this humanism of love, born from the revolution that has radically altered the family since the Middle Ages, produces what I call a *second republican idea*, which broadens and reconstructs on a new basis the first republicanism, the republicanism of law and Enlightenment, of effort on behalf of one's native country, a republicanism at once revolutionary (or reformist) and nationalist, embodied first by the Jacobins, then by great men such as Jules Ferry or Clemenceau and still a source of inspiration for *souverainiste*[2] politicians, on the Right as well as on the Left.

The three failings of the first humanism

If we are really to understand the need for this second humanism, we need to grasp, as is hardly ever done, what is lacking in the first humanism and inevitably leads it into unacceptable contradictions. It's a question whose full extent I realized only quite recently. For a long time, I was a republican in the 'first manner', an heir of the Enlightenment, of Voltaire, of the Encyclopaedists and Kant. Only with my book *Man Made God: The Meaning of Life* did I really start to perceive the need for a second humanism, a humanism of love, a humanism that can't be reduced to the rationalist philosophy of the Enlightenment on the one hand and human rights or the republican idea on the other.

How is the first humanism or, if you prefer (it boils down to the same thing), the first modern republicanism (let's leave Rome out of this) spoiled by three grave failings that, far from being just an accidental blip, appear as an inevitable, indeed essential consequence of its entire project? We can see the damage wrought by it throughout the nineteenth and twentieth centuries with the stupefying gap between the universalist principles of human rights and, within the very framework of the republican idea, the Terror in the French Revolution, the maintenance and even the development of slavery and the violence of colonization. How can we explain the unjust exactions, the reign of brute force, the massacres that led to millions of deaths in the name of the republican ideal or, at least, to deaths that it was powerless to stop?

Claude Capelier: We'd need to add the appalling contradiction that affected the status granted to women. The Declaration of the Rights of Man and the Citizen applies, in principle, to women as well as to men and should have led to equality in the condition of the two sexes, an equality that would start to be realized only two centuries later!

---

[2] Adherents of *souverainisme* support local and regional autonomy and often a degree of protectionism; they tend to be Eurosceptics and to promote a 'Europe of the nations'. In France, they are mainly right-wing, but some (such as the Citizen and Republic Movement) are on the Left.

Luc Ferry: That's perfectly true, but I was starting with the way human rights were flouted within the framework of the republican idea. They led not simply to injustice but to acts of terror and extermination – to crimes against humanity. As a follow-up to your remarks, I'll merely say that for a long time, in certain manuals of history or political science, people explained – and in some cases perhaps they still do – that universal suffrage was established in France in 1848! But this is false, since only universal suffrage *for men* was granted. As everyone knows, only in the second half of the twentieth century did votes for women gradually become a reality in our European democracies. Indeed, in Switzerland, despite being a modern, European and democratic country (in some ways, actually, much more democratic than France), the last canton to grant the vote to women did so only in April 1991!

Let's get back to our guiding thread – the violent disparity between the ideals that were proclaimed and the reality of their application. Contrary to what most hardline republicans say these days, this disparity isn't just the contingent, anecdotal effect of 'the weight of history', the consequence of what is also these days called the 'spirit of the age', which – it is claimed – merely delayed the implementation of sublime principles; as we shall see, it was also the result of grave failings in the conception of the republican idea itself. However, everything got off to a good start with the Revolution – for instance with the sublime promises of the Declaration of the Rights of Man that lie at the heart of our republican idea.

The heart of the 'French-style' republican idea: the human being has rights, quite irrespective of all the ways he is rooted in a community

Before detailing the three essential deficiencies of the first republicanism, we need to say, however briefly, how the republican conception of 'French-style' human rights was originally both laden with promises and quite grandiose. What lay at the heart of the declaration of 1789 was the *abstract humanism* from which a universal emancipation, applicable to humanity as a whole, was expected. The word 'abstract' should here be understood in its strongest meaning, in the etymological sense of the term: in this 1789 declaration – which is very different, for example, from the American version of 1776 – it is stated that the human being has rights and deserves to be respected, *quite irrespective of [abstraction faite de]* all the ways he is rooted in a community. The French revolutionaries no longer considered the human being as a *member* of a social *body* – and the biological metaphors here are remarkable – but as an individual who is capable of abstracting himself, of freeing himself from every form of belonging to a community, whether in the religious, ethnic, linguistic, cultural or even national and patriotic sense. It's the idea that the human being, even 'naked', seen outside any community, must be respected and protected. Hence the reaction of the counter-revolutionaries. People always mention, as particularly emblematic, the words of de Maistre that illustrate their rejection of this conception of man based on his freedom alone. Let me quote from memory: 'In my life I have seen Frenchmen, Italians and Russians; I even know, thanks to Montesquieu, that one can be a Persian; but as for "man", I declare that I have never met one in my life; if he exists, I am quite ignorant of the fact.' Edmund Burke said the same thing in England: he knew of the rights of Germans, Englishmen or Frenchmen, but he was unacquainted with the rights of man since he did not know of man in general.

This idea of abstract humanism, full of grandeur and promise, turns out to lie behind our conception of republican secularism, too, since it means that the human being, in his freedom, has the power but also the right to emancipate himself from all the groups to which he might belong, including religious groups. As Rabaut Saint-Étienne put it: 'Our history is not our code.' Our history is not like some kind of computer programme, which we are forced to obey and obliged to repeat.

What is the freedom of the first humanism? It is this ability to tear ourselves away from all the codes that claim to define us, to dictate our destinies, whether these codes are the codes of nature or history. Basically, it's a form of anti-determinism: it's the idea that the human being is free in the sense that he or she is not prisoner of any natural or biological, sociological or historical determinism. This doesn't mean that the human being isn't 'in situation', as Sartre put it: we are men or women, that much is undeniable, we are also born into a society, an epoch, a language and a culture, into a social milieu – all of this is self-evident. However, there's a difference between 'being in a definite situation' and 'being defined by this situation': circumstances may constrain us, but for as long as we are alive we are never completely their plaything. We have a margin of manoeuvre to twist circumstances to our own aims, or to free ourselves from their grip. This is the fine, and profound, notion of freedom that lies behind the French-style republican idea.

The double historicity of mankind

This definition of freedom, understood as the ability to tear ourselves away from the given, had already made an appearance in the Renaissance, especially in the magnificent *Oration on the Dignity of Man* by Pico della Mirandola (1486), but it did not reach its full development until Rousseau, in his *Discourse on the Origins of Inequality*. Its first consequence – we'll be seeing shortly how it also lies behind a certain colonialism – was a definition of the human being as a being of historicity. If we aren't prisoners of an eternal, ahistorical human nature, it's because we can, through our freedom, forge our destiny, make our own history. Man, thanks to his freedom, was thus represented as the subject of a double historicity, as has been luminously shown by Alexis Philonenko, in his fine preface to Kant's *On Education*, where he says that *the human being, unlike the animal who is ruled from all eternity and for ever by his natural instinct, is characterized by a double history – the history of the individual (this is called education) and the collective history of the species (this is called culture and politics)*. While the little sea turtle, guided by nature, can do everything once it's emerged from the egg – walk, swim, eat – without any help from its parents, the human baby needs a very long individual history to be raised, educated and instructed. A humorous way of summing up the situation would be to say that, unlike the little sea turtle, the human child stays at home until the age of twenty-five. Such is the historicity of education!

As for the second historicity, that of the species, which entails the incessant transformation of societies, the succession of political events and the evolution of civilizations, it will bear the memory of each generation so as to lead men to build up a world that will increasingly be their own work and less and less subjected to natural constraints. While animal societies, guided by nature, are always the same (termite heaps, ants' nests, beehives do not change after tens of thousands of years, at least unless the biological evolution of the species entails new variations), Paris, London and New York change every ten years, and even more every century; over a period of five hundred or a thousand years, these cities become completely unrecognizable since, as Rousseau puts it, the human being is, thanks to his freedom, the 'perfectible' being, the being of history.

This extremely profound idea lies behind all of modern politics, or at least all republican politics: the human being is a perfectible being, a free and historical being, since within him, as Rousseau puts it in a formula that every republican can make his own, 'the will still speaks even when nature is silent'.

Why the first humanism broke some of its promises

How are we to explain, given all this, that such magnificent conceptions have been able to produce or accept the terrifying consequences described above (the revolutionary Terror, slavery, colonization)? What is wrong with the republican idea? As I have stated, in spite of its real attachment to liberty, equality and fraternity – in spite of the rights of man – it also produced three new principles that led it to suspend the nobility of the initial founding values: nationalism; the revolutionary idea; and, finally, a racism of a particular kind which lay behind the colonial gaze, linked to the idea that if history and progress are the supreme mark of man's 'greatness', everything that is not part and parcel of the logic of innovation can be regarded as 'backward', 'under-developed', 'primitive' and thus inferior.

Let's go through these points in succession, from the simplest to the most profound.

The three constitutive weaknesses of the republican idea: nationalism, the revolutionary idea and the colonial gaze

The trap of nationalism

The first reason which impelled our republicans to suspend the ideals of the rights of man was nationalism. In the name of the national, patriotic ideal, they actually went so far as to justify and practise, if not slavery, at least its logical corollary: a colonization whose initial steps were of unprecedented brutality. This was because the 'greatness of France' appeared as a goal higher than all others, including the goal of ensuring that there was no excuse for alienating the fundamental rights of man – which had been proclaimed inalienable. This comes across very clearly in certain texts by Tocqueville that are, in this respect, both surprising and instructive. In *Democracy in America*, he may have shown himself to be the greatest and most intelligent opponent of slavery; he seems to have forgotten all his principles in the case of Algeria, where he became a fierce supporter of the most atrocious colonization as carried out under General Bugeaud.

How can this double language be understood? It obviously stems from the fact that, in the case of America, Tocqueville was faithful to his principles, while when it came to Algeria, the national idea, which was making a comeback, meant that in his view the aforesaid principles could be sidelined in the higher interests of the nation. In spite of all this, it would be difficult to envisage a thinker of his calibre falling prey to such a gross contradiction out of pure opportunism. In fact, there is another reason – one that was, in his view, decisive: in a historical period in which he could see an advance in the democratic feelings of a society tending towards equality (a guarantee of passions that in his opinion were peaceable but mediocre), he thought that the only transcendence to have survived in a world now centred on individuals was that of the nation. The sole sacrificial object, the sole meaningful aim that still had any grandeur in politics, was the national idea.

If we compare *Democracy in America* with the writings that the same Alexis de Tocqueville produced on colonization in Algeria, we are bound to be staggered. It's like Dr Tocqueville and Mr Hyde! The former is a sublime abolitionist; the second, a cynical supporter of General Bugeaud, who utters inflammatory speeches to his greater glory, against the philanthropists who denounced the crimes committed in Algeria and emphasized that the end did not justify the means. However, the Tocqueville of *Democracy in America* who denounces the slavery of the blacks and considers that the Indians have been treated appallingly does a complete about-face as soon as it becomes a question of France's higher interests in North Africa. He gives unstinting support to the war crimes committed by the French army in Algeria in the 1840s, even in their most abominable aspects: starving populations to death by burning their harvests, destroying and pillaging villages, separating mothers from their children, exterminating the Algerians in their hundreds by lighting fires in the caves in which they had taken shelter.

Tzvetan Todorov had the excellent idea of publishing these disquieting but fascinating texts in which Tocqueville defends French conquests in North Africa in his book *De la colonie en Algérie*. In it, we find some, alas, all too evocative titles: 'What kind of war can and should be made on the Arabs'; 'On the means used to wage war economically with the fewest possible losses' (these means were the ones used by Bugeaud that I've just mentioned). There is a complete contrast between this and the passage in *Democracy in America* called 'Against colonial, slave-owning Eurocentrism' in which we read the following: 'Could we not say, in view of what is happening in the world, that the European is to men of other races what man himself is to animals?' In *Democracy in America*, I should emphasize, Tocqueville is completely hostile to Eurocentrism: he condemns, in the firmest terms, the way Europeans have behaved towards Indian populations or those of African origin. 'The success of the Cherokees,' he writes, 'proves that Indians are able to civilize themselves.' And he is absolutely opposed to slavery: 'Christianity is a religion of free men. In the Christian idea, all men are born free and equal,' so that the Declaration of the Rights of Man strikes him quite rightly as a secularization of the idea of Christian equality as expressed in the Parable of the Talents:

> It is we Europeans who have given a definite, practical meaning to the Christian idea that all men are born equal and have applied it to the facts of this world. It is we who, destroying throughout the world the principle of castes, of classes, in rediscovering, as has been said, the lost title deeds of the human race, it is we who, by spreading across the whole universe the notion of the equality of men before the law, just as Christianity had created the idea of the equality of all men before God, I say it is we who are the real authors of the abolition of slavery.

A fine meditation, establishing as it does, with considerable subtlety, a line of descent from the Christian heritage to the republican idea: equality before God is transposed into equality before the law.

What Todorov very clearly shows, in his presentation of these texts, is that the speeches where Tocqueville seems to be abjuring his highest convictions, uttering words that, these days, would belong in a court of law, are possible only because they refer to a transcendent principle, that of the nation – a principle that strikes him as so evidently superior that it justifies the suspension of the rights of man: 'We should aim first and foremost at ensuring that these independent Arabs become accustomed to seeing us involved in their interior affairs. Colonization without domination will always, in my view, be an incomplete and precarious business.' Or this: 'We initially recognized that we were not facing a real army, but the population itself. We had less to vanquish a government than to repress a people.' Whereupon, Tocqueville waxes indignant when he sees any signs of indulgence or, worse, of benevolence towards the 'natives': 'In certain places, instead of reserving for Europeans the most fertile, best watered, best prepared lands possessed by this domain, we have given them to the natives.' This was scandalous, in his view. And he goes on to defend Bugeaud's whole politics:

It is of little account to cross mountains and to beat the mountain-dwellers once or twice – we need to attack their interests. We cannot do this by speeding through like an arrow; we need to come down hard on the territory of every tribe. We need to take measures to have enough supplies to stay there sufficient time to destroy the villages, cut the fruit trees, burn or pull up the harvests, empty the grain stores, search the ravines, rocks and caves to seize women, children, herds and movables: only thus can we force these proud mountain dwellers to capitulate. In addition, I have often heard it being said in France, by men whom I respect, but with whom I do not agree, that it was wrong to burn harvests, to empty grain stores and indeed to seize defenceless men, women, and children. These are, in my view, unfortunate necessities, but any people that wishes to wage war on the Arabs will be obliged to submit to them.

I am quoting this at length, since it is fascinating to see such an intelligent man writing on the one hand the finest texts for the abolition of slavery, and, on the other, the most abject apologia for what we would these days consider to be war crimes against the populations of North Africa. Indeed, he derives this rather unusual conception of ethnology from it: 'One can study barbarian peoples only with weapons in hand!'

The chronic degradation of the revolutionary ideal

The same perversions, *mutatis mutandis*, undermine the revolutionary tradition. Where the patriotic idea suspends human rights abroad, the revolutionary idea abolishes them on the national territory itself. In France, this happened in 1793 with the Terror. The war in the Vendée unquestionably gave rise to a real genocide which caused hundreds of thousands of deaths. Even apart from the ravages of the guillotine, historians such as Pierre Chaunu have discovered evidence describing revolutionaries smashing the skulls of aristocrats' children against the walls of their chateau, or forcing their parents to jump from the galleries onto halberds or pikes held by soldiers. These practices were not really in keeping with the ideal of the rights of man that was being brandished at the same time. Victor Hugo depicted such scenes with great power in his novel *Ninety-Three*. French revolutionary episodes are as often as not extremely violent: this was the case in 1848 too, and again during the Paris Commune (whether we are talking about the revolution or the counter-revolution).

Like the nation for Tocqueville, the revolution was a principle of transcendence for the revolutionaries, a great sacrificial cause that in their view was of more significance than the promises made to the individual whose rights, in these conditions, were of little worth. The decay of revolutionary ideals, like those of nationalism, is inherent in the particular forms of transcendence that tacitly sustain them. A major part of the history of Europe and its epigones, throughout the world, bears the fruits but also the wounds of these degraded ideals. As we know, the transposition of the revolutionary idea to the communist countries created over a hundred million deaths.

Now it is in its very essence, in the way it was constructed, that the republican idea was – at least in its first versions – both nationalist and revolutionary. It included the supporters of Hébert and of Babeuf, the great Jacobins, and the great theorists of the national revolution, such as Sieyès. And this explains why, even today, we find a republicanism of the Right, often drawing on Gaullist support against the liberals, and a republicanism of the Left, which is also opposed to the liberal wing (the 'second Left') in its own camp.

Indeed, over and above nationalism and the idea of revolution, the republican ideal includes within it, right from the start, an almost 'natural' propensity to a certain colonial racism.

An essential propensity to cultural racism secretly undermines the republican conception of history

Nobody who is not prey to blatant bad faith can be unaware of the extent to which nationalism and the idea of revolution have led to the suspension of human rights. However, people are all too happy to conclude that their excesses are committed by extremists blinded by their ideology, while in reality nationalism and the revolutionary idea lie at the heart of the republican idea. And the absolute kernel of this idea conceals another poison, much more subtle and all the more dangerous. It lies behind what, in the career of Jules Ferry, initially appears so contradictory and yet is completely consistent – we shall soon see why. Jules Ferry was simultaneously the prime defender of republican education and the greatest theorist of colonization. And yet he is not a right-wing thinker like Tocqueville, nor a revolutionary armed with a knife between his teeth, but a moderate figure of the republican Left. How are we to explain this apparent paradox?

In order to understand it, we need to start out again from the republican conception of history based on the logic of human perfectibility – the freedom through which the human being is deemed able to tear himself away from natural and social 'codes', 'from his race and his social class'. It is through this freedom, as we have seen, that he enters a history fully oriented towards the idea of progress, whether we are talking of individual progress – self-education – or the collective progress of the sciences, the arts, political institutions, social equity and everyday customs. What could be finer or more inspiring? And yet it is at the very root of this grandiose project, the emblem of everything that appears best in European civilization, that is distilled the poison I mentioned just now: for if the republican conception of history and progress appears to be a characteristic – essential in the full meaning of the term – of mankind, one almost inevitable result is that traditional societies, societies without history, those, that is, that are organized around respect for customs, for elders and ancestors, in short, around respect for the past and not the cult of the future, inevitably appear *inferior*. For an authentic republican, of course, this does not mean that they are inferior 'by nature' (this form of 'biologistic' racism is in principle excluded from republican thought, imbued as it is with the idea that man can always tear himself away from nature), but that those 'unfortunate' beings, 'abandoned by history', have to be educated, if need be from outside and by force! In this sense, Jules Ferry had – as is clearly revealed in his writings – the conviction that he was, in colonization, pursuing the same educative project that he was drawing up for the children of France. Hence those notorious phrases about 'our ancestors the Gauls' trotted out in front of pupils from overseas who were unlikely to have had distant ancestors in the region of Gergovie.[3]

These republican colonizers thus came up against a problem that we can understand these days with the help of Lévi-Strauss and the birth of modern ethnology but that in those days they had little means of grasping: if the essence of man is historicity, where do we place those whom we consider to be excluded from that history? If 'African man has not entered history', as a now notorious speech delivered by President Sarkozy in Dakar put it, how can we fail to be tempted to bring him into that history, if not by force, at least from the outside? Let's eliminate, as far as we can, the ambiguities that, on this subject, are all the more difficult to resolve on that they go to the very heart of our democratic passions. It is clear that the peoples of Africa entered history long ago. And the ethnologists have taught us how much the societies that Lévi-Strauss calls 'savage' evolve over time. So long as we keep these two evident facts in sight, we have to admit that there is nothing scandalous in claiming that 'traditional societies have not entered history'; this, indeed, is exactly what anthropologists such as Pierre Clastres or Claude Lévi-Strauss would say about them. What is essential to these societies is that, so long as they remain exclusively attached to their cultural model, they reject what we Europeans call historicity, i.e., the modern logic of

---

[3] Near Clermont-Ferrand: the site of Vercingetorix's victory over Julius Caesar in 52 BC.

permanent innovation, of a ceaseless breaking away from tradition. Clastres and Lévi-Strauss emphasize the fact that these societies are, unlike ours, entirely organized around ancestral customs, in other words, around the past. They are just not oriented towards any future project: as Clastres shows, there are cases where any Guayaki chief who tried to introduce some innovation was put to death.

So, from the French Revolution onwards, we see a gap opening up between two types of society: on the one hand, those that place value entirely in respect for ancient customs, for the tradition transmitted by ancestors and ultimately rooted in the gods; on the other, those that resolutely extol permanent innovation, breaking away from the past, progress and an orientation to the future. Traditional societies honour the elderly, in whom they see the witnesses of an immutable civilization; to the same degree, societies which are forever reinventing themselves indulge in a cult of youth, seen as bearing the future.

From this angle, nineteenth-century republicans, who identify civilization with a history turned to the future and entirely devoted to innovation and progress, could not see the traditional societies of the peoples they set off to colonize in Africa as communities that are, at best, still a little *infra-human*, or at any event infantile since they are without writing and 'without history' (in the sense they give that word). Of course, as we now know, and as it is worth repeating, traditional societies change over time and, from this point of view, they do have a history. The fact remains that they seem not to have the same *desire* for history and innovation that sets apart the societies that our republicans consider to be the only truly 'civilized' ones; they are focused on the past and the mythic origins of the law, on the maintenance of ancient customs, while European societies are structurally turned towards the future into which they project their inexhaustible thirst for change. In this regard, the connection between an absence of writing and an absence of history is extremely powerful: while it is possible to give an oral rendition of tales, legends and myths, even ancient ones, a historical science can only be constituted, *stricto sensu*, by writing, in the form of archives which provide direct evidence of former ages, allow evidence to be compared and interpretations to be criticized, and thus enable the development of objective thinking. All of this, of course, is missing in traditional societies without writing which are thus regarded, by the colonizer, as 'primitive'.

They are thus considered – sometimes, indeed, with the best intentions in the world, but more often with less noble ulterior motives – as incapable of making any progress by themselves, as not having sufficient autonomy to attain it. So the 'civilized' republic claims the right to 'educate the barbarian' 'from the outside'. This makes it easier to understand why it was no coincidence that Jules Ferry was both educator and colonist. It was a matter of 'raising' the 'natives', or – to use the eloquent term – the 'naturals [*les naturels*]' – in the sense of 'educating' them if you're a republican, or of 'raising them' (as if for food) if you're a racist, to provide them, from outside, with civilization, the only form of civilization that exists, to derive profit from them.

We can see how the republican idea, however much it seems linked to the Left, leads to the same result as the patriotic idea on the Right: to violence and colonization.

How we moved from the first to the second humanism which led to our breaking with colonial racism

So the rot has set in. The very foundation of the republican idea as it emerged from the first humanism is infected by an essential 'vice', by a 'faulty conception' that leads to the variant of cultural racism that colonization so violently puts into practice. Some people raised their voices, as I have mentioned, against the infringements not only of human rights but, even more simply, of the most elementary feelings of humanity. However pusillanimous they may have been, they have contributed to a gradual awareness of the need to establish less flagrantly unjust relations with the colonized peoples. However, we need to remember the way the vast majority of French people still talked about the colonized peoples when I was a child – there are countless examples in literature, in cartoons, in advertising and in films – to grasp the extent to which the first style of republican thinking was unable to silence its own demons.

So how was the shift from the first to the second humanism effected? How did people move on from colonial imperialism to aid for development, to mention one symbolic example? Let's avoid one potentially very serious misunderstanding: the second humanism has not in the slightest denied the idea of freedom as an ability to free mankind from natural or social determinants; it does not in the least dispute the most fundamental principle of the republican idea, nor the rights of man, nor the Enlightenment, nor the rationalist ideal. *Instead of adding to this principle nationalist or revolutionary forms of transcendence* that tend to suspend the grandiose aspects of the revolution of the Enlightenment, *it opens up the dimension of love, the humanitarian concern for others and the interest in future generations, in the shape of sympathy* ('*sympathos*', 'suffering with'), *thanks to which there will be a move – and this is highly symbolic in itself – from colonization to public aid for development* – which is really not the same thing and marks a huge break.

The advent of the second humanism, borne by the revolution in the modern family, thus entails the emergence of a new figure in human rights or, if you prefer, a new relation to human rights: humanitarian action. In a way that is very striking but perfectly understandable after what we have seen, *the development of a modernist and secular form of humanitarianism, whose origin goes back to the creation of the Red Cross by Henri Dunant, runs absolutely parallel, historically speaking, with the growth in influence of the modern family.* Why? Very simply because the love that holds sway in the families whose *raison d'être* it has become arouses, to an ever-increasing extent, a new feeling towards distant otherness, to one's neighbour [in the Biblical sense: *le prochain*] and not just those who are nearest [*le proche*]. The feeling of sympathy I mentioned developed gradually between 1850 and 1960, after which it grew exponentially: we can see the results today with, for example, the rise of charity work. It is well worth observing the extent to which participation in charitable actions has developed in the working and less well-off classes, who are well aware of the problem, as opposed to the intellectual elites who often consider it with a certain disdain.

The formula of Robert Badinter that I quoted above ('do not let be done to others what you would not wish to be done to you or to anyone else') can be applied to the sphere of charity work as well as to humanitarian action. *In this sense, it really adds a new dimension to human rights – a dimension based on feeling.*

We are no longer, as with Kant, in the domain of an ethics of respect but already in an ethics of love which in many ways (we'll come back to this) links back to the Sermon on the Mount, notably the passage where Christ declares to the Orthodox Jews that he has not come 'to abolish the law, but to fulfil it' – love being precisely this 'fulfilment' of law. With the humanitarian sphere, in other words with the right to interfere, we thus see a move outside the limits of the national framework deemed, in the first humanism, to be an indispensable intermediary if concrete shape were to be given to human rights which were, let us recall, initially the rights of the citizen and thus, in spite of everything, the rights of a member of a particular nation.

The humanitarian sphere, as I said, is first and foremost the struggle against indifference; but this combat became possible only as a result of the spread of love within families. Thus we see that, far from being opposed to one another, the private sphere and the public sphere, the intimate and the universal, are interrelated today more than ever before: *the revolution of love is also an ethical and political revolution.*

The 'deconstruction' of traditional values permitted the advent of charitable and humanitarian action and of a politics turned towards future generations

Claude Capelier: It seems to me that there's a missing link in your description of the move from the humanism of reason to the humanism of love, of the emergence – through charitable or humanitarian action – of an active dimension in human rights, based on feeling. For us to be 'in sympathy' with the problems of people that the 'first-style' republicans serenely ignored, the 'deconstruction' of traditional values (in everyday customs, in the arts and even in politics) first had to emancipate and enhance forms of existence to which we are now sensitive.

Luc Ferry: You're completely right. We didn't move, just like that, straight from the first republican idea to the second, from the humanism of right and reason to the humanism of concern and sympathy for the other, just as we didn't move from the, let's call it, traditional art of the novel à la Balzac or Stendhal to the novels of Milan Kundera or Philip Roth: we'll come back to this when we tackle the question of art. In both cases, there was an intermediary, called 'deconstruction'. In this respect, deconstruction, whose impostures I have often criticized, especially in modern art or what I've called the 'thought of the sixties', had – in spite of everything and often unwittingly – certain positive effects.

Claude Capelier: It's also deconstruction that now enables us to recognize, in peoples who have a culture very different from ours, the obvious fact that they are our equals and that otherness, connected with the difference of cultures, is a source of enrichment, not a justification of imperialism.

Luc Ferry: The deconstruction of the illusions of traditional metaphysics was accomplished, in the wake of Nietzsche and Heidegger, in the name of the recognition of 'difference' and otherness. This certainly impelled the Europeans, at long last, to understand – unlike the first republicans – that these 'first peoples' (*peuples premiers*) are not some kind of children to whom, as Jules Ferry thought, education needs to be brought 'from outside', but that they also possess their own civilizations and cultures. As everyone knows, indeed, in the history of art, what was then known as *art nègre* (proof that there was still a long way to go!) would be an important source of cubism and of modern art in its beginnings.

Staying with the subject of our present reflections (the contribution of deconstruction to the advent of a humanism of love), we need to realize that there are two moments in deconstruction: the 'Lévi-Strauss moment' which, in order to eradicate any possible kind of justification of colonialism, lays it down that each civilization has a value incommensurable with the others, thereby issuing in a complete relativism; and the 'Foucault–Deleuze–Derrida' moment which, so to speak, generalized out from this to every particular of human existence, to all the 'differences' and all the 'dissonances', so as to promote the allegedly irreducible singularity of 'becoming-woman', of 'becoming-homosexual', of the 'subject of madness', and so on.

The Lévi-Strauss moment: the critique of ethnocentrism and the birth of a radical relativism

The 'Lévi-Strauss moment' was that of a decentring, a critique of ethnocentrism and Eurocentrism. In 1956, in *Race and History*, Lévi-Strauss gave a radical formulation of the new approach to the diversity of civilizations that was emerging at the time: Europe was not the only civilization, the societies that were still being called primitive and that Lévi-Strauss called 'savage societies' were not worth less than the others; they were not inferior, they were just 'different'. They were not 'underdeveloped'; they had a different culture from ours. The project of ethnology was no longer to analyse civilizations in terms of hierarchy, on a scale measuring their degree of success in relation to a European model, but to study them in their irreducible otherness.

It must be said that circumstances made a change of perspective necessary. In the days after the Second World War, it appeared that Europe, which had previously been identified with the Enlightenment and with civilization as such, had been, in reality, the Europe of imperialism abroad and of Nazism or fascism at home – not just in Germany and Italy, but in Vichy France, in Spain, in Portugal, in Romania, Croatia, and so on. This, indeed, explains why in France all intellectuals, more or less, were communists or close to communism, from Furet to Morin via Foucault, Althusser and Le Roy Ladurie.

Lévi-Strauss yielded to the conviction that, in order to avoid once and for all the hierarchization implied by Eurocentrism, we need to fight tooth and nail to defend a total relativism. All cultures and all civilizations are equally valuable. He thus quite rightly broke away from the hitherto constant habit of studying other civilizations in accordance with the criteria of our own; but, from another angle, his absolute relativism led him, as we shall see, to unacceptable conclusions. In spite of the unquestionable contribution of his work, he pushes his relativist logic so far that he ends up maintaining paradoxes whose absurdity undermines the rest of his positions. An interview published in *Le Figaro* of 22 July 1989 brings out this slippage with astonishing clarity. So what does he say? The journalist asks him – with Hitler and Nazism explicitly in his sights – whether Nazi barbarity meant the end of a civilization (German or European civilization).

Here is Lévi-Strauss's reply:

> *Lévi-Strauss*: No, the advent of barbarism does not entail the end of civilization. What you designate as barbarism, from the point of a civilization, is civilization. It's always the other who is the barbarian.
>
> *Le Figaro*: But in this case we're talking about Hitlerism.
>
> *Lévi-Strauss*: But *they* thought they were civilization. Imagine they won, since it's easy enough to imagine.
>
> *Le Figaro*: There would have been a barbarian order.
>
> *Lévi-Strauss*: An order that we call barbarian and for them would have been a great civilization.
>
> *Le Figaro*: Based on the destruction of others.
>
> *Lévi-Strauss*: Yes, even if the Jews had been wiped from the face of the earth (I'm adopting the hypothesis of a triumph of Hitlerism), what does that matter in relation to hundreds of millennia or millions of years? These are things that must have happened a certain number of times in the history of mankind. If we look at this period with the curiosity of an ethnologist, the only attitude to take is to say to oneself, well, a catastrophe befell a fraction of the mankind of which I am part, and that's all. It's very disagreeable for people who are Jewish, but ...

Unfortunately (or fortunately), the journalist stops the ethnologist right there, but you can guess the rest: genocide is disagreeable for the Jews, of course, but this is basically just a detail in terms of the long duration [*longue durée*], one vicissitude among others in the grand scheme of history. Uttered by anyone other than Lévi-Strauss, these remarks would certainly have brought a judicial sentence on their author. However, I wouldn't dream of accusing the father of structuralism of anti-Semitism here. What he had in mind was the massacre of the Indians, the genocide perpetrated by those colonists who committed such vile acts as spreading through the forest clothes contaminated by smallpox which they knew to be deadly to the natives. What lay behind Lévi-Strauss's words was rather self-hatred, a sacred horror of the Europe that he identified with the misdeeds of colonization, of the ethnocentrism that arrogantly took itself to be the *sole* civilization and allowed itself, in the name of this 'superiority', to destroy other peoples and other cultures. He thought that, in order to change the point of view, in order to make a clean break with imperialism, it was necessary to affirm what I might call an *absolute* relativism – and it was this conviction, in its most extreme form, which led Lévi-Strauss to explain serenely to a journalist who obviously could not believe his ears that, if Nazism had won out over the democratic powers, it might have appeared as a great civilization. It's just a question of different viewpoints between which no overall perspective allows us to judge: in the eyes of the historian or the ethnologist, it's all one.

Not only do I not share this opinion but, to be frank, and with all due respect, I find it abhorrent. To make things worse, for all its faults, I view European civilization, in certain respects that I am going to specify, as the most admirable of all. However, relativism is hardy, deeply anchored in people's minds and thus especially difficult to denounce in that it obliges anyone who sets out to criticize it to go against the flow of his age. If I dispute the idea that everything's the same, that Nazism and democracy are exact equivalents, if I state that certain civilizations are therefore superior to others (note that Lévi-Strauss uses the word 'civilization', not 'society', 'culture' or 'political regime'), won't I myself be immediately accused of succumbing to the Eurocentrism or even the racism that have left such a mark – and this cannot be denied – on the history of Europe in its relations with colonized peoples? Obviously, I don't accept this, but it's not easy to escape the trap laid by the dominant ideology that relativism has become.

To achieve this, I first need to make clear what is meant by 'great civilization'. I'll offer a simple answer: a great civilization is a civilization that moves beyond its particular identity, that addresses a message to mankind as a whole, that gives it something precious, something that changes – if only partly – the course of world history. In this sense, the Chinese, Arab-Moslem and Indian civilizations, to take just these three examples, are great civilizations: each of them bears treasures which mark mankind for good, for example, algebra, Confucianism or the *Mahabharata*. In addition, in our school textbooks, the expression 'great civilization', despite the fact that it implicitly contains a certain notion of hierarchy, is used to designate them without this arousing the least polemic. It is also obvious that European society deserves to be considered great for its scientific, aesthetic and even political creations. In every conservatoire in the world, Bach and Mozart are played. From Beijing to Moooow, via Madras and Algiers, people study Plato, Rousseau and Shakespeare. However, none of these civilizations is innocent of atrocities such as those pointed out by Lévi-Strauss. Europe – and who would dream of denying it? – was not just the Europe of Newton and Einstein, of Beethoven and Stravinsky, of Hugo and Kant, of Vermeer and Cézanne, of democracy and human rights. It was also Nazism, slavery, colonization, Stalinism – in which, be it said straight away to avoid any misunderstanding, if all civilizations are not equal, not all is equal within one and the same civilization, either.

So why give one's vote to Europe? Out of Eurocentrism? Not at all, but because this old continent of ours invented something unique and precious, something singular and grandiose: a culture of the autonomy of the individual unmatched by any other, a demand that we think by ourselves, that we leave, as Kant said in regard to the Enlightenment, the infantile 'minority' in which all religious civilizations, all theocracies and all authoritarian regimes have so far maintained mankind. This was already the meaning, as Hegel saw, of the wonderful aesthetic revolution embodied in Dutch painting of the seventeenth century. For the first time in the history of mankind, works of an at last 'secular' nature were called upon to represent everyday scenes, the simplest and most humdrum moments in the ordinary lives of human beings themselves anonymous. The people represented no longer belong necessarily to Greek mythology or sacred history. Nor are they 'great men', the heroes of famous battles, illustrious personages, kings, princes, noble or wealthy characters, but mere humans, grasped in the most clearly profane instants of the day. Human beings start to emerge from heteronomy, from the representation of higher religious or cosmological principles from outside mankind, and this move towards autonomy sketched out in art infiltrates the whole of European civilization, from (rationalist) philosophy to (secular and democratic) politics via science (hostile to clerical dogmas) and private life (where marriage for love replaces the marriage of convenience imposed by parents and villages). Such is the genius of a Europe that, of its own volition, finally abolished slavery and colonization and shed itself of totalitarian regimes – in short, recognized otherness. Nothing, in this extolling of European civilization, implies the least racism, the least neo-colonial inclination. It simply reflects the idea that if everything is of equal worth, nothing is worth anything.

Hence the ambiguities of the 'intellectual decolonization' represented by deconstruction in its Lévi-Strauss moment: it sets out from a just and sympathetic set of values, and its critique of the first humanism, of the first colonialist republicanism, is relevant. But the relativism that it sets up in place to achieve these aims ends up being absurd.

The making sacred of difference and otherness: the 'Foucault–Derrida' moment

After the 'Lévi-Strauss moment', we entered what I labelled the 'Foucault–Derrida moment', or what we might call the philosophies of *différance*. These heirs of Nietzsche and Heidegger developed a form of 'deconstruction' distinct from that of Lévi-Strauss in its principles and its aims, but even more radical in its critique and in the positions it set out. They pursued the 'deconstruction' of Eurocentric imperialism (of the 'humanist *episteme*' and of 'phallogocentrism') as the political face of the humanist 'metaphysics of subjectivity'; they also, at the same time, pursued the deconstruction of everything which, in the history of mankind and especially of Europe, contributed to the repression (in their view) of dimensions of life which they wished to liberate: 'sexual orientations' in all their diversity, marginality in all its forms – the madman, women, animals, gays, and so on. We mentioned the liberation of women above, but we should also mention the liberation of homosexuals: if women have been dominated for many millennia, homosexuals have been ostracized, despised and condemned in even more violent ways. They were victims of a real terror during the Hitler period when the Nazis deported and exterminated them. And, faced with such a monstrous repression, there was an urgent need to break down prejudices, to push the critique right into the foundations of the European civilization that had tolerated them, and to propose an alternative way of thinking that would give their due to all *differences*, all forms of otherness, all minorities, all diversities – I'm using several synonyms to make myself clear.

We are therefore going to move from the *ethnological relativism* of Lévi-Strauss to *philosophies of difference*, carrying forward the heritage of Nietzsche and Heidegger. It will no longer just be a question, as in Lévi-Strauss, of respecting and preserving each civilization as a singular and incomparable variant of the human predisposition to 'form a society' but of cultivating the differences that can singularize human beings in every area: so we are going to ensure that we deepen these singularities, that we develop our 'becoming-woman', our 'becoming-homosexual', or even our 'becoming-schizophrenic'.

It was indeed with a *History of Madness* that Foucault embarked on his critique of western rationality and, in particular, Cartesianism. He questioned the modern norms in whose name, in his view, everything irrational was rejected outside the bounds of humanity, starting with madness: the mad were locked up inside the walls of the asylum. I have elsewhere explained – inspired by the analyses of Marcel Gauchet – why Foucault's ideas about the lunatic asylums and the treatment of madness are, in my view, quite wrong. But that's not the point; they interest me here only as a symptom of this history of deconstruction. Like Lévi-Strauss, he had the right intentions when he started out, but his conclusion turned out to be wrong and sometimes perfectly absurd. Where he was right was in his view that Europe did indeed relegate everything that was 'other', everything that was 'different', if not by enclosing it in asylums and prisons, at least by confining it within the grid of a purportedly universal hierarchy in the name of which anything that diverged from the norm systematically risked being marginalized or repressed – with colonization providing a perfect illustration of this relegation, though the treatment of homosexuality was in certain ways a similar case. It's worth remembering that, right up until the 1990s, the World Health Organization still defined it as a 'perversion' or an 'illness'.

Thus, in the second half of the twentieth century, we witnessed a double deconstruction of the Eurocentrism inherited from the Enlightenment – in other words, a deconstruction of the first republican humanism, carried out in the name of ethnological relativism on the one hand and, on the other, in the name of philosophies of difference. And, as was the case for ethnological relativism, the philosophies of difference may initially have helped to tear away the Eurocentric blinkers – and this enabled them to meet with considerable success in the United States, at a time when the movements for the liberation of minorities (especially of the blacks) were really taking off, and could therefore find the intellectual weapons for their struggles in the work of Derrida and Foucault. But these philosophies of difference then went further, driven by their own momentum to, as it were, 'o'erleap' themselves and fall on the other side. Their aim had been to free us from the shackles of the first humanism but they ended up clapping us back in the chains of our natural and social particularisms, entrapping us in our singularities, transforming communitarian impulses into new prisons. On the justified pretext that the first republican humanism limited the recognition of otherness and the expression of singularity, the philosophies of difference proceeded to encourage women to emphasize the particularities of their 'nature', communities to preserve their specific characteristics, and the mentally ill to cultivate their pathological traits. The result was that difference, far from being liberated, became a new barracks. The aim had been a great liberation: in the end, people became the willing prisoners of their nature or their social group.

Just as radical ethnological relativism had led Lévi-Strauss, out of a desire for complete consistency, to embrace the absurd position in which Nazism and democracy were as good as each other – something which nobody, not even he, ever seriously thought – the republican idea was, in the wake of 1968, literally blown to pieces once the possibility of legitimate common values had been denied. This was the origin of the most radical 'pupil-centred' ideas: recognizing the child's 'otherness' in its irreducible singularity led to leaving his upbringing entirely in his own hands, sometimes completely. And this was done in the name of the right to difference and the recognition of otherness.

The decay of 'philosophies of difference': from struggles for liberation to the communitarian retreat

In my book *The New Ecological Order*, I quoted a text that I'd like to mention again here as it seems to me so symptomatic of the trap into which fall those who, having correctly criticized the shortcomings of humanism, end up, as the phrase has it, 'throwing the baby out with the bathwater'. It's an article that was very typical of the spirit of the times, written for the review *Autogestion*, the weekly of the Parti Socialiste Unifié (the party of Michel Rocard, and of what was in those days called the 'second Left').[4] It was signed by two authors who teamed up for the occasion: Daniel Cohn-Bendit, whose career is notorious, and Félix Guattari, known for his collaboration with Gilles Deleuze in the wake of the philosophies of difference. Here is an extract (I have to admit that every time I read it, I'm torn between laughter and pity):

> The aim is not to achieve some approximate consensus on a few general statements covering the set of current problems, but quite the opposite: to foster what we call a culture of '*dissensus*' that strives to extend particular positions and re-singularize human individuals and groups. How dumb it would be to try and get immigrants, feminists, rock enthusiasts, regionalists, pacifists, ecologists and IT freaks to agree on one single vision of things!

Here, the idea of a *res publica* falls apart. Guattari explains his ideas further in one of his books:

> The different levels of practices not only should not be homogenized, made consistent under some transcendent supervision: rather, they need to be caught up in processes of heterogenesis. Never will feminists be sufficiently involved in a becoming-woman, and there is no reason to ask immigrants to abandon the cultural features that are part and parcel of their being or their membership of a national group [*leur appartenance nationalitaire*].

The 'cultural features that are part and parcel of their being': sorry, but this is all but intolerable. It marks the point where the extreme Left, by making sacred the right to difference, joins the most abhorrent extreme right in its refusal of any freedom, any possibility for individuals to break away from the conditions in which they are born. This is the polar opposite of what was, for all its faults, the best thing about the first humanism, namely, the

---

[4] The *deuxième gauche* was a spectrum of left-wing groups in France, active from the 1950s, united by their opposition to totalitarianism.

hypothesis of human freedom understood as a faculty for transcending all categorizations. It's no coincidence if, on this shared anti-republican basis, the extreme Left and the new Right later both shared a hostility (for identical reasons and with a similar zeal) towards, for example, the law banning evident religious signs in schools.

Claude Capelier: 'Deconstruction' aspired to free us from anything that hampered the free expression of our potentialities but, by attacking everything that could hold back our spontaneity, it ended up by ruling out any possibility of our rising above the immediately given to transform it or break away from it: and this was how it was paradoxically brought back, unwittingly, to the starting point of the whole effort of liberation – that initial moment when we are still subject to the set of biological dispositions and social circumstances that determine us. Those who attempt to take this to its logical conclusion end up in a desperate mess: if we have to abstain from asking anyone to 'abandon the cultural features that are part and parcel of their being', this comes down to saying that we have no right to try and put a stop to female circumcision, for example. This would of course be appalling. So much for liberation!

Luc Ferry: Exactly. The consequence is that the 'immigrant' is imprisoned in the prison of his origins instead of being offered a bilingual, bicultural status that would be a real opportunity for him. And then, close on the heels of this, we find the policies of positive discrimination: the 'right to difference' is transformed into 'a difference in rights'. The ideology of the right to difference, which was historically an ideology of the extreme Right, and at the very least counter-revolutionary, now belongs to the extreme Left.

The hollow debate between 'old' republicans and 'modernists'

We can also see from this how there is something profoundly right and at the same time something rather terrifying in 'deconstruction'. This poses a huge problem which is far from being merely theoretical: it has far-reaching consequences for our political lives since this situation leads the protagonists in the debate over education or immigration to get stuck in an absurd antinomy: on the one hand, we have the philosophers of difference and their epigones failing to see that their supposedly liberating aspirations risk leading to the complete opposite of what they imagined, namely the imprisoning of each person in his or her difference, community and historical or 'natural' particularities; on the other, the republicans merely fall back on an appeal for the restoration of the values and civic life of bygone days, without realizing that the heritage of May 68 would never have been able to flourish unless republicanism itself had been riddled right from the start by certain formal defects, starting with the three that I've just mentioned: fundamentalist nationalism, the terrorist revolutionary ideal and cultural racism. Any step backwards, any 'restoration', is impossible: hence my own philosophical project, which consists in unearthing and building up the foundations of a new humanism that will reconcile the best aspects of the first (freedom, rights, reason, a focus on the universal and on the common good, secularism) and the contributions – quite negative in their results, but legitimate in their aims – of deconstruction. I've stated why what I call the humanism of love, as a finally non-'metaphysical' humanism, seemed in my view to fulfil these requirements.

Claude Capelier: Those who profess to be 'old' republicans these days actually seem to me to be much more 'modernist' than they affect to believe: they always give me the impression of 'playing' at 'being Jules Ferry' (which was certainly not the case of their model) rather than of endeavouring, as he did, to build up the republic of the future. They're filled with nostalgia, rather than participating actively in progress; they're filled with *pathos*, with emotion rather than with inventive reason; they are critical, rather than constructive. For the great republicans of history, transcendence was progress and the happiness that it would bring to the people; transcendence, for today's republicans, is the memory of the republic of Jules Ferry! What could be less 'humanist in the first manner'? This is a republic for the democracies ruled by popular opinion: a sentimental pose of indignation in which a dreamed-of past enables them to lay down the law for everyone without needing to give an example in one's own deeds. At best, it's a way of 'deconstructing' modernity by carrying out a recent and imaginary reconstruction of our history: our republicans are modernists despite themselves.

Luc Ferry: That's why I sometimes find it so hard to get my message across to republicans, Gaullists or *souverainistes*. They include some remarkable people, for whom I have feelings of esteem and friendship, but you need only listen to them talking about education, for example, to realize the huge gap there is between current realities and the educational ideal they defend. If the school system for which they are so nostalgic had been as perfect and well adapted for today's children as they imagine, it would never have vanished. If it has changed, this is because there were reasons for it to do so. Since I agree with them in considering that the excesses of 'pupil-centred teaching' have caused terrible damage, and since, like them, I think that there's a need for systematic exercises, for intensive engagement with reading and writing, for a greater stress on the teaching of great works of literature, and so on, they think I'm a supporter of their other ideas. I find it extremely difficult to explain to them that, in spite of the points we have in common, we differ on the essential things: I'm convinced, as I'll explain in more detail in the next chapter, that the revolution of love means we need to integrate into education hitherto neglected forms of reflection and approaches to culture: the 'pupil-centred' thinkers have given an inadequate and sometimes harmful answer to a good question.

It's worth repeating that any step backwards is impossible; restoration is always foolish or catastrophic. You can act to transform a situation, but you can't stop it having become what it is. No restoration has ever worked, and it never will: only a complete lack of historical awareness will prevent you realizing as much. And the republicans I have in mind are too intelligent not to know this. When they rehabilitate the wearing of traditional grey smocks in school, or the china inkwells filled with purple ink (I'm hardly exaggerating), when they set out to restore traditional authority and a liking for hard work, and so on, they know perfectly well that their speeches and writings will actually change nothing. Hence their profoundly nostalgic and pessimistic side. There is a joy in pessimism, and this is their fundamental pathos: 'Ah! I know that nobody listens to me, but luckily I'm here to keep the flame of the republican idea burning – here I stand, a lonely martyr to the rising tide of American money-grubbing, etc., etc.' This is a pose that can draw on the plus sides of pessimism, which can give wings to the critical spirit and even to writing, breathing fire into its style.

The humanism of love reintroduces the sacred and the long-term perspective into politics

The humanism of love will, as I've said, enable us to move beyond (in other words, to incorporate and reconstruct on a wider base) the essential contributions of republicanism and deconstruction. Since it is founded on love, it opens up – and we have seen why – onto the problematic of future generations: this gives new depth to the long-term perspective and for the first time, in a completely new shape (quite unlike the great nationalist and revolutionary causes), gives a value to the collective sacrifices that cannot be avoided at times of crisis – a value that is not death-dealing. I must insist on this, as it's a truly vital point: I am not talking here about a sacrifice that involves mass death: it is not a sacrifice on behalf of the Nation or the Revolution, for entities that are external to and higher than humanity. Rather, it is a sacrifice on behalf of what is human [*l'humain*]. For the first time in history, we are witnessing the emergence of a principle of meaning that, even though it justifies a long-term action and sacrifices, is not in itself a sacrificial ideology destined to kill huge numbers of people. The only sacrifices for which it calls are those carried out by human beings on behalf of human beings – not for great causes that have always led to the extermination of vast swathes of mankind.

Of course, I have friends on the right who look back with nostalgia on the patriotic idea, and who miss the time when generations of young people were ready to die for their countries; and I have other friends on the Left who look back with nostalgia on the revolutionary utopias, the times when the Red Guard would decimate whole populations in the name of the masses. I say to them: for pity's sake! Please! The fact that those murderous tomfooleries, those monstrous lunacies, have finally vanished from our lives is the best news not just of the century, but of the millennium! Champagne all round!

Claude Capelier: If someone sacrifices himself for his children, it's because he loves them more than anything else in the world, and in this sense he's sacrificing himself for his own sake. In humanitarian actions, we find, in a less absolute guise, something of the same kind. In my view, these examples give some idea of what you mean by the idea of a 'sacrifice that is not death-dealing'.

Luc Ferry: The theorists of 'sympathy', at the end of the eighteenth and beginning of the nineteenth centuries, had come up with a very fine analysis of this aspect of moral feelings: you never lose yourself in a sacrifice to which you consent out of sympathy. Furthermore, they showed – correctly, in my view – that a good man cannot be entirely happy when others are not, at least (and this much is certain) when those he loves are not happy. This is perhaps not real virtue, at least not in Kant's sense but, after all, it's the best we can hope for in the area of collective and political life: when ethics and self-interest are pointing in the same direction, who's going to complain?

Two 'received ideas' prevent people from becoming aware of the revolution of love

I have the impression that what I am saying about the second humanism ought to be understood by everyone, by philosophers and by those who've never studied philosophy. And I can see from the lectures I give pretty much across the world that this is quite often the case. However, I sometimes also realize that the revolution of love, whose manifestations I am simply trying to describe, identifying its causes and grasping its meaning, doesn't always appear so clear to the 'elites', let's say those in the political and intellectual worlds, while it seems more convincing to a non-'specialized' audience.

If my diagnostic is indeed correct, I think that two ideas, generally accepted for so long that nobody would now dream of questioning them, prevent people from becoming aware of the huge changes we are living through. Firstly, there is the conviction that the public sphere is and must remain radically separate from the private sphere. And second is the theory that politics is defined exclusively by the management of individual interests. Any truth in these two theses is only at a very superficial level: indeed, they turn out to be completely wrong if you get to the bottom of the matter. In any case, they are what stops many intellectuals and politicians these days from perceiving the full extent of the upheaval represented by the emergence of the second humanism.

To begin with, marriage and family, in their view, fall entirely within private life: they conclude from this that the changes that occur in them, however considerable, can be of concern only to the intimate sphere. So they never realize that they have a collective dimension. And yet this dimension is obvious: how can anyone imagine that a revolution that affects all individuals has, in a democracy, no repercussions on the collective level? It's absurd: the very universality of the change brought about by the shift from a marriage of convenience to a marriage of love already turns it into a completely collective phenomenon, a 'total social phenomenon' as the sociologists would call it – and it is hard to see how a phenomenon which spares nobody would not have an impact on common aspirations!

The other day, someone objected to my position and said that 'marriage is not a political project'! Frankly, faced with such a monumental lack of understanding, I was left speechless. Love for one's children is not a political project either. Might I point out that this fact has not escaped my notice? However, this type of remark, which completely misses my point, does enable me to gauge the total perplexity and the errors to which it may give rise. So let's try, if possible, to be more clear. Obviously, I'm not saying that loving one's children is going to replace the revolutionary idea or the national idea. I'd be a complete fool if I proffered such asinine observations! I'm simply saying that, while the revolution of love is initially brought about in private life, it continues to find reflection on the collective, public and political level. This reflection can be observed in the sphere of the family, of course, which is already something more inclusive than that of the individual but, over and above even that, in the sphere of art and of politics, with the new problematic of future generations.

As we have seen, it is this problematic that gives a political meaning to the idea of sacrifice, and my claim is that this idea can now be accepted only on two conditions. First, we need to know *on behalf of whom* we are required to devote our efforts and not just *on behalf of what*. Second, the sacrifices which we agree to make must be made with a full guarantee of transparency and equity. Thus we move away from abstract, death-dealing causes (the nation, the revolution) to our neighbours or to people near to us (in other words, people who are anonymous or geographically distant, those on which humanitarian efforts focus). So from henceforth we can on the basis of this analysis identify the two guidelines of a future politics. For whom will we be making sacrifices? And on what conditions, and with what guarantees of equity will we do so? In my view, these are the two keys of the politics to come.

Another objection is quite often raised, especially by those who are still attached to old political notions, to revolutionary utopias, for example: the world we are entering, they point out, doesn't need care bears! I speak of love, and that's really nice, but people are really rather angry about the greed of the banks, the selfishness of the financial world, the arrogance of the powerful, the existence of inequality, and so on.

This, too, is a complete misunderstanding. First, because the opposite of love is, of course, hatred, and I would not dream of denying the existence of hatred in today's world. Its weight is obvious and indeed crushing, not merely in the wars which shed so much blood throughout the world, but in everyday life, political and professional, in the world of the media in particular, which is structurally turned towards what is going wrong, arousing scandal and indignation. All this is self-evident and only a blind man could deny it. The question I'm raising has nothing to do with such a negation but simply with this: *if politics must in principle aim at the general interest, the common good, on what must it be based to achieve this, to mobilize people? On the national or revolutionary idea? I don't think so: as I've said, they are, if not dead, at least stale ideas, and I'm glad they are. On the other hand – yes, I'm convinced of it: if we base our great objectives on concern for the future of our young people, rooting this concern as much as possible in families and surrounding it with all the most credible guarantees of equity, it is possible to drag a country out of a crisis and mobilize the energy necessary to do this. Hatred, selfishness and all the defects in the world that you may care to mention obviously don't just vanish because the principle of love now guides families. But if we rely on this principle, we can probably get past all that lies in the way of our quest for the common good.*

In my view, there's nothing naive or conciliatory about this, just the clear awareness that democratic passions aren't, as Hobbes and, later, Tocqueville thought, inevitably all rather dismal: they cannot be reduced to fear, jealousy and anger. Fraternity, too, can play a role, so long as it is not reduced only to the benefits of national health insurance and the welfare state, but viewed as a real emotional bond, too, the bond that exists in families or between friends, when one of life's accidents happens to disturb or shatter your existence ...

If I may summarize while taking the argument a stage further, I'd say that the two major political theories that have dominated Europe for two centuries, namely liberalism and socialism (Marxism included), have two fundamental characteristics in common which have largely stood in the way of the understanding of what I've just been saying.

In the first place, they thought, as we've seen, that whatever is part of private life is, and must remain, completely outside the political field. This seems self-evident, and yet it's wrong: the revolution of love is the best illustration of this. If it's just a matter of saying that we mustn't intrude on the private lives of politicians or their affairs, I'm obviously in agreement: when the international press 'took up residence in Bill Clinton's underpants' (as Alain Finkielkraut aptly put it), I was, like any man of decency, scandalized by this voyeurism, with its mixture of resentment and smutty-minded puritanism – a voyeurism all the more nauseating for being passed off as democracy at its best.

This is not, of course, what I'm talking about: the point I'm trying to bring out is that revolutions in private life have a huge impact on political life. May 68 is a clear example: this was neither a political revolution (witness the fact that the Constitution of 1958 is still in force), nor an economic revolution (contrary to what Marxists hoped for, liberal capitalism is more arrogant than ever, which shows how little impact May 68 had in this area). On the other hand, the 'events' did bring about a spectacular, many-sided and enduring revolution in lifestyle.

Now a revolution in lifestyle by definition affects both the private *and* the collective realms inseparably. Indeed, in the wake of this lifestyle revolution, political issues, practices and achievements were considerably modified. Ecological themes became more important in every sector of opinion; the policy of aid for those in difficulty (the unemployed, the sick, the elderly, pupils with special needs, etc.) became more varied and personalized; and there was a questioning of hierarchies, with the result that those in power are now obliged to justify their decisions continually. And so on.

The great error of liberalism, as of Marxism, was to have confined everything concerning private life to 'civil society', as if this latter expression – which is common to both Marxists and liberals – served only to deprive the realities it designates of any political dimension.

The second error they have in common is that they reduce politics to what André Comte-Sponville called, in our debate – see the book we co-authored, *La Sagesse des Modernes* (*The Wisdom of the Moderns*) – the 'management of interests'. This is a mistaken and reductive view of politics. The latter is not limited to a quest for the general interest as a compromise between or harmonization of private interests; or, more exactly, if the general interest is indeed its aim, the passions are involved and are indeed indispensable for its realization. You need to be blind not to see that politics is first and foremost a matter of passions. This is what traditional politics did not manage to understand: passions are much more powerful in history than are interests. Passions – be they nationalist, religious or revolutionary, whether they stem from jealousy, anger or indignation – as we can see these days play a far more significant role in the great social upheavals than does the rational quest to satisfy 'properly understood' interests. If human beings sought their interests rationally, everyone would know about it. Quite probably, not a single war would have taken place, since it is hardly ever really in anyone's interest to wage war; it is passion that impels us to do so. If human beings were rational as methodological individualism and ordinary Marxism both imagine, they would always find a compromise. Hence we can see that it is the passions which lead the world, and not our interests.

The democratic passions

The genius of Tocqueville (who, from this point of view, does not entirely fit the mould of traditional liberal theories) lay in his grasping the fact that there were 'democratic passions': among these, of course, could be found anger and fear, as Hobbes had already seen, but even more envy and jealousy, which lie at the origin of the resentment known as indignation and which are very far from having any comparable influence in the aristocratic world. The more one lives in an egalitarian world, the more widespread jealousy becomes. We are really jealous only of people who are close to us. It is within a single profession that rivalries are fomented. Journalists hate each other: the same applies to politicians, intellectuals, singers, actors, academics, and so on. As Tocqueville explains (and as John Rawls also said), democracy, more than any other regime, makes different degrees of success intolerable because one person outdoes the rest, even though everyone is deemed to set out from the same level. 'Why's he such a success, and not me, when we do the same job and we started out with the same chances?' Then we make up justifications and consoling reasons, even resorting to the most mean-spirited arguments: if he's a success, it's 'because he's a whore who appears on TV', 'because he knows the right people', 'because his works are facile and vulgar', 'because he's part of a lobby', and so on. Then we make every excuse for ourselves, we make up the most wrongheaded explanations so as to lessen the pain we feel at the idea that the other is a bigger success, is richer, has a prettier wife or is more popular. The logic behind all this is rather dire, but it clearly illustrates how the democratic passions dominate.

However, Tocqueville, like Hobbes before him, in putting his finger on the passion of fear (in his view a fundamental one), forgot one essential dimension in his great and eloquent analysis of the passions: the democratic passions are not simply dismal, mediocre passions. What I have added to this tradition of analysis of the interests and the passions is the fact that there is one collectively and sociologically new passion, namely love, which is found in different types of feeling, including sympathy. To repeat my previous point: love has always existed but, before the triumph of marriage for love, it did not have the now central role it plays as the major bond within the family and society.

Claude Capelier: Love wasn't the foundational value of the basic cell that the family represents for society; now that it has become so, its influence spreads out from families to the collective and finally appears as the fundamental value of the social world as a whole and its organization.

Luc Ferry: Yes, that's a good way of putting it. Over and above indignation, anger and jealousy, which are in my view hateful passions, love has become the strongest passion and the most widespread in our lives. This is the element I have added to the analyses of Tocqueville, analyses which are very profound but incomplete – which is of course only to be expected, given the fact that in his day, the modern family wasn't yet in existence. In this sense, we can say that love has largely become a democratic passion, at least just as much as anger, indignation and jealousy.

Claude Capelier: It goes without saying, but, as they say, it's probably better to say it all the same: there's no way we are going back over the difference between the 'liberty of the ancients' and the 'liberty of the moderns' as Benjamin Constant put it: nobody wants to limit the autonomy of private life – quite the opposite, in fact. There's no question of indulging in totalitarian and even less in sentimental politics. It's just that private values have moved into the heart of public issues. Policies are being developed on health, education, support for the elderly, ecology – and people now expect public action to seek (even when it doesn't succeed as much as one might wish) to take into account all the means that enable individuals to flourish and realize themselves most fully. This change in political aims is one illustration of what you call the 'revolution of love'. Apart from all of this, which is still a bit general, what more concrete political effects should, in your view, accompany the upheavals that are taking place?

From the revolution of love to the question of the future of Europe

Luc Ferry: Of course, this is not the place to set out a detailed programme that would aim to cover each of the major ministerial departments. I'm not going to start discussing VAT, or this or that measure designed to fight unemployment or reform public services. However, if what I've been saying so far has been understood, it will be easy to deduce that the fundamental political question is that of the future of Europe, in so far as Europe is the bearer of a civilization – a singular and precious civilization – of autonomy. It's not just political autonomy that I have in mind, not just the invention of democracy and human rights. It is also the civilization in which art and culture have emancipated themselves from the authority of religion: this can be seen, for example, in the fabulous revolution represented by Dutch seventeenth-century painting, which, for the first time in the history of mankind, produced pictures that were emancipated from any religious or cosmological subject and could devote themselves to the depiction of daily life, of the human as such. This staging of daily life, of human life as such, is the prime example of the ideal of autonomy that has increasingly characterized Europe throughout its history.

So, unlike Lévi-Strauss, I believe that, *on this level*, Europe is a superior civilization to all others: it bestowed on mankind an unparalleled culture of autonomy. This autonomy is, of course, partly political. 'Freedom is obedience to the law one has laid down for oneself,' as Rousseau put it. This is the republican and democratic principle that we have embodied. Europe is also the application of human rights even if, as we have said often enough, it was also slavery, colonization and fascism. Europe, above all, is the civilization of the counter-culture: we abolished slavery of our own volition, not because we had lost a war. And Europe is finally, as I mentioned above, the continent in which humans were for the first time treated as adults and not as children. There is a superiority of Europe in the field of autonomy and adulthood on the political and cultural levels, but also on the level of private life. The shift from the arranged marriage to the love marriage is autonomy itself. This is the best example of the culture of autonomy, and nobody can deny that this historical phenomenon was born in Europe, even if it extends more or less throughout the rest of the world. The question of the survival or, if we prefer less pessimistic terms, the flourishing of European civilization, is thus in my view the most crucial of political questions, and the crisis we are experiencing today makes it more urgent than ever.

So let's try and speak about it in more concrete terms.

There are two ways of interpreting the current crisis. Actually, it's wrong to call it a 'crisis', as it's a structural problem from which it is not clear that we can really 'emerge'.

The first interpretation is essentially that of the liberals: it can be found, for instance, in Angela Merkel's speeches. She emphasizes budgetary restrictions, the reduction of debt and other deficits. In her view, what has pushed us old European countries into a crisis of sovereign debt is the logic of demagogy. With wide-ranging electoral promises, we've built up expenses we can't finance, and that's why we're so heavily in debt: at present, France's debts total over 1,700 billion euros. So we've practically handed ourselves over, bound and gagged, to the tender mercies of the ratings agencies and the financial markets. From this point of view, insulating these markets and criticizing the financial world is about as smart as insulting a tiger shark that comes to gobble you up because you've gone for a swim in shark-infested waters: it's completely pointless. Financial markets aren't personal beings that we can wag a moralizing finger at. If we want to emerge from the crisis, we need to apply the 'golden rule' rigorously – return to a strict budgetary balance that enables us to pay off our debts. QED.

The problem with this reading of things is that paying off our debts is practically impossible without growth, especially if the rates of interest in the debtor countries explode because the ratings agencies have downgraded them. Hence the relative credibility of a completely different interpretation of the crisis.

It seems the complete converse, in fact, because it suggests that debt is absolutely not the cause of our difficulties. Far from it! It's a good thing, say the republican *souverainistes* (on the Right and on the Left), that we've got into debt since otherwise we'd have undermined both growth and the social fabric. At present, there are eight million people in France living on less than 900 euros per month, according to the latest figures from INSEE, the National Institute for Statistics: if we hadn't got into debt, if we hadn't pursued social policies financed by borrowing, if the social shock absorbers had been made less flexible, not only would we have undermined what little growth still existed, we'd also have created an unendurable amount of suffering among the population, with the risk of a violent backlash that would inevitably have weakened our economy even further.

So what is the real reason for the crisis, if not debt? It is – claim the proponents of this thesis – the absence of any European economic, social and financial policy, of which the independence of the European Central Bank is the perfect symbol. Why, you may ask, should this European Union deprived of any economic or political leadership, which has performed rather satisfactorily for thirty or forty years, now be doomed to failure, unless it reforms itself from top to bottom? Because the situation is different: the BRIC countries (Brazil, Russia, India and China, along with others) have entered the western-style circuit of consumption and production. China, in particular, now has a threefold dumping effect on our economies that is becoming untenable and unmanageable for our old welfare states. Firstly, economic dumping: the production costs of Chinese businesses are on average twenty-five times lower than ours. Then there is social dumping: in China, there is no welfare state, no social policy, no trades unions and no independent political parties. Finally, there is a monetary dumping: the yuan is apparently undervalued by 50 per cent in relation to the euro. Europe is powerless to fight against this threefold dumping because it deliberately refuses to create any common policy to be imposed on member states.

Thus we find ourselves completely at a loss in the face of competition from two and a half billion Indians and Chinese who are emerging from poverty – and one can only be glad on their behalf! – but who are now quite unfairly rivalling us. Furthermore, the European Central Bank is obliged, by the treaties that guaranteed its independence and set out its objectives, to stick to decisions that have only a slender relationship with current necessities: in the best case, it needs to come up with complex and legally debatable solutions to ward off the most insistent challenges. The solutions aimed at aiding the most heavily indebted countries are, as everyone knows, not enough to save them, especially as rigorous measures plunge them into recession. So we are on the edge of the abyss.

The fact of the matter is that both these interpretations are overall correct. Of course, it is debt that has led us to hand ourselves over to the financial markets and the ratings agencies, but we also need to accept that there are reasons why we have got into debt. Without economic growth and without any social and monetary policy, we will not reduce the deficit. It won't be reduced, or at least not only or even mainly, by limiting state expenditure.

This question may appear purely material, economic or political in the most tactical sense of the term, but in reality it's a question of the survival of Europe as a civilization. Christian Saint-Étienne has written a short book in which he suggests setting up, within the European Community, a new political entity composed of nine countries which would provide themselves with a common economic government and a 'federal euro'. In this restricted Europe, the different states would stop competing, especially on the fiscal and financial level. As Saint-Étienne puts it: California is richer than Germany, Alabama is poorer than Portugal, but adjustment operates at the level of the federal budget, of the American state, without anyone even raising any questions. Likewise, it's absurd to imagine that Greece will become an industrial country (it will always be, as long as humans are around, a land of service industries and tourism). Like the adjustment carried out between the different states in America, or between the different regions in France, we need to ensure that resources are transferred from the richest to the poorest European states, which means that their fiscal systems need to be harmonized and the competition between them in this domain halted. This can't be done in a Europe of 27 countries. Hence the idea of creating within it an authentically federal Europe of nine members, with the Franco-German couple, Spain, Portugal, Benelux, Austria and Italy. As Saint-Étienne emphasizes, history shows that no currency can survive for long unless there is some sovereign power behind it. Once this nine-member federal Europe has been constituted, it would need to follow simultaneously a policy of the golden rule, a policy of debt elimination within each state and a policy of growth. The latter would need to be based, as Jacques Attali has been recommending for many a year without gaining a hearing, on the issuing of 'euro-bonds' and on massive borrowing. (This has little sense in the French context, but is necessary on the European level where there will be sufficient economic power for this rise in debt not to be a synonym for increasing weakness.)

A solution such as this, though it meets with the approval of most serious economists, probably has no chance of being put into practice 'out of the blue', due to the different kinds of inertia that will inevitably thwart its implementation. However, if the crisis should suddenly worsen, which unfortunately is all too probable, it is easy to imagine that heads of state will prefer to run the risk of taking this historic step rather than abandoning themselves, and their populations with them, to the inevitable shipwreck.

What is at issue, after all, is the European project as a whole, the project without which the culture of autonomy that we mentioned just now may well disappear. And even here, to draw a connection with the revolution of love, it's the whole question of the future of generations to come that is being raised. In future generations, do we want this Europe of the culture of autonomy to continue existing and to blossom, or do we want it to vanish? What is at stake is the preservation and flourishing of a model that can be put forward for the rest of the world to follow – and we ourselves need to say clearly whether we are committed to it or not. If we don't say we are, then yes, the *souverainistes* will carry the day, the euro will break up and that will be the end of the European project. It will be a catastrophe, not on the economic level (at least not only that), but mainly on the intellectual, moral and political levels. We will see the return of nationalism and, from then on, our history will be one of decline.

3

On the Spiritual in Art and Education

Luc Ferry: We've just seen how the new roles played by love in the private sphere were reflected in the public sphere, with the result that the political field was completely refigured, gradually emancipating itself from the old sacrificial causes, the Nation and the Revolution, and focusing instead on the future of coming generations. It might be thought that upbringing and, even more, education would be less affected by this new principle of meaning, given the weight of the inherited traditions on which they are based and which they help to transmit; but as we shall see, in fact, the humanism of love reorganizes them from top to bottom, while at the same time opening up new dimensions in them. This chapter devoted to spiritual life in education and art will also help us better understand, as it were 'from within', how the public aspects and the intimate aspects of love combine in these areas that are, each in their own way, at the turning point of the individual and the collective.

Upbringing and education in the age of the second humanism

Before getting to the nub of the matter, I'd like to make two pre-liminary remarks. They are necessary, in my view, if I am to avoid creating the conciliatory impression that everything is for the best in the best of all possible worlds, which is of course largely untrue: as for a couple, even if we rate it as the highest thing of all, love raises at least as many problems in upbringing as it solves, if not more.

Love raises as many questions as it solves

Romantic love, as I have said, is at once what drives the modern couple and what renders it fragile – it is the main reason why two people get together and the main cause of divorce. Furthermore, and I would emphasize this too, it is easily transformed into its opposite, hatred: thus it is probably more difficult to get human beings to live together when passion has become their dominant character trait and one of their main aspirations than was the case, for example, when the logic of interests was more important than any other consideration. The same is true when it comes to upbringing. Invoking love as the new principle for the family is no reason for relapsing into naivety and deciding that it makes everything wonderful and easy. In many respects, it makes our lives much more complicated, and it is doubtless in the pedagogic domain that this complexity is most evident. Here it plays a role that is at once essential, almost vital, but also tremendously disruptive. In short, for upbringing as for the couple, love is as much the difficulty as it is the solution.

From upbringing to education

My second remark is this: it is crucial, when discussing these questions, to draw a clear distinction that is all too often forgotten: that between *upbringing* and *education*. In principle, *upbringing* is the business of parents, a relation between them and their children. *Education*, on the other hand, is the task not of the parents but of *teachers*, and it is not aimed at children in all dimensions of their personality but at *pupils*. Parents/children/upbringing, teachers/pupils/education: the words have a meaning, and it's better not to get them mixed up. Teachers are not the parents of our children and this is not their job – in any case, they have no wish to be so. Conversely, it is not desirable for parents to become too involved in the education which their children receive in the classroom. It can of course happen that parents decide to take over the responsibility of educating their children, but this is an exception and it makes no change to the principle at stake: upbringing and education imply different types of relation between the adults who take on these tasks and the children who benefit. Of course, the problems of upbringing and of education respectively are closely linked. Sometimes they overlap, with parents helping their children to do their homework, and teachers occasionally giving a few moral pointers to undisciplined pupils – but this doesn't mean they are the same.

This may seem self-evident, but it's no longer quite so evident these days, when certain parents rely more and more on the school to give their children an upbringing that they themselves are unable or unwilling to provide. And yet it would be more than desirable, let us say straight away, for children to be brought up *before* they start school and that teachers be largely absolved of the tasks linked to upbringing properly speaking. Even if education necessarily involves an element of upbringing, they need to be able to concentrate first and foremost on the transmission of knowledge. Most of the problems we encounter these days in education stem from the confusion between these two registers, or, to put it more clearly: education suffers greatly if a child's upbringing *before* it starts school has been defective. Now this defect is largely linked to the rise of an excessively sentimental love of children in families, of an emotional atmosphere that is sometimes so intense that it destroys the minimum of parental authority without which no training in civility is possible. Hence it is obvious that love, when it is excessive, overwhelming, undisciplined, uncontrolled or troublesome, is sometimes a problem rather than a solution.

Let's see why.

The three dimensions, Christian, Jewish and Greek, of European upbringing: love, the Law and works

We succeed in bringing up our children properly (as opposed to 'educating' them) when we manage to transmit to them love, law, and works. This is what I call the Christian, Jewish and Greek elements, respectively. If I am here basing my remarks on European examples, this is not out of any Eurocentrism. If I were Iraqi or

Chinese, I'd find other examples without difficulty, but as I'm talking about a phenomenon that springs from Europe and as I am focusing on upbringing as we practise it here, I am using examples that are our points of reference. Why love, law and works?

As far as *love* is concerned, I am drawing on what all the good psychiatrists and psychoanalysts say these days: when children do not feel that they have been loved adequately, they are made more vulnerable. The love that we give them, that we pass on to them, enables them to acquire, in their adult lives, 'self-esteem' – the ability that Boris Cyrulnik calls 'resilience', without which nobody can face up to life's unforeseen events. Resilience in physics is the ability of a dented solid object to reassume its initial shape. For human beings, it's the capacity to bounce back after life's upsets, after sudden catastrophes or even, more simply, to face the obstacles and difficulties that we inevitably encounter in the course of our lives. Even though things don't of course happen so mechanically, the general validity of this principle can be accepted: the more a child has been loved, the more self-confident it will be, the more it will be endowed with a certain self-esteem that will give it the extra strength to overcome setbacks and obstacles. We here find, at least to begin with, the fundamental element of Christianity: the passing on of love. And this lies at the heart of everything that nowadays founds the meaning of our lives: the modern family is a family in which, in the vast majority of cases, not only do we love our children, we actually *worship* them – which Christianity, as we all know, would not recommend ('worship God alone').

The second element, just as fundamental, is *law*. This is what Lacan, in his own jargon, called the dimension of the 'symbolic', of which the Law of Moses is, to some extent, the archetype. If I am here using Judaism as my point of reference, this is because it is a religion of the Law. This doesn't at all mean that it's not just as much a religion of love: there is a very fine philosophy of love in Judaism. Nonetheless, what we retain of it in Europe, culturally speaking, is first and foremost the glorification of that Law which children must respect because it is the Law, without always asking the question 'Why?' Just because! The Law, that law which you can't argue with, which you can't negotiate with your children, on the principle that our 'no' must be a no and our 'yes' a yes, is what enables them to enter social life [*la vie de la cité*] or, put more simply, the space of civility. Unless we hand the Law on to them, we make them uncivil, and in extreme cases we push them into a marginal existence, or even into madness. We deprive them of the means of living in harmony with other people. Love is not enough: we need the Jewish element of the Law to ensure our children will behave properly and have peaceable relations with other people, *including those they don't like* or even those they hate and with whom they should nonetheless avoid going to war and giving in to violence. In this, unlike what the ideologies of May 68 claimed, with their celebrated and stupid 'it is forbidden to forbid', no upbringing can manage without the law.

Finally, there are *works*. This is what I call the Greek element, for it was the Greeks who, essentially, invented the literary 'genres' around which our culture is structured: they drew distinctions between the first great philosophical, literary, poetic, scientific, dramatic (and so forth) works. Unless we hand on fundamental knowledge to our children, knowledge that is like a treasure hidden in the great works, we are not 'equipping' them, if I may say so, to deal with the sometimes unlikely, often tumultuous and varied life that awaits them in our democratic societies stripped of their traditions.

Handing on love, Law and works: you will now understand why I said this was the definition of a successful upbringing. Let me say again that I'm here talking of upbringing, not education, even if the third element obviously affects education too.

Love tends these days to imperil respect for the Law and the knowledge of works

These days, under the impact of the revolution in the meaning of life of which it comprises the very heart, love tends literally to 'devour' Law and knowledge. We love our children so much, we love them with such a passion, with a sentimentality that is sometimes so excessive, that far too often we are unable to hand on to them the authority of the Law, or to make them work hard enough to ensure that they have fully picked up the knowledge that is fundamental. A historical comparison would show our children up in a harsh light. We need only think of the 90-page essays that Nietzsche, at the age of just fifteen, wrote to his fellow pupils at high school, in Greek if you please, on the comparative merits of Sophocles and Euripides, to gauge how much our children, however intelligent they might be, have lost the capacity for hard work when compared with the good pupils of bygone centuries. Actually, writing in Greek doesn't require any particular intelligence – all Greeks, even the dumbest, could do so! But for a young German or French pupil of the nineteenth century, it meant an amount of work that would be quite unimaginable these days. Most of Hegel's *Phenomenology of Spirit* was a course aimed at pupils also aged about fifteen! Schelling wrote his first works at nineteen: none of our children, however brilliant, would be able to write at the same age a hundredth part of what he wrote on the basis of a knowledge of Kant and Fichte that is also unimaginable for today's students. Note that I'm not referring here to genius or even talent, simply to the quantity of work. When you take a close look at the library of books that young Romantics such as Hugo, Gautier, Nodier or Nerval had already absorbed by the time our children are taking the baccalaureate, you can't help feeling that, in spite of all the love we have for them (or rather, as we shall see, because of it), the decline in the capacity for work, but also in the motivations that underlay it, is really quite alarming even if we can see that, conversely, young people today have access to an incomparably wider range of information, experiences and ideas than that to which previous generations were limited.

It's a fact directly connected with the revolution of love: we love our children so much that we are unable to make them work as hard as they should to become cultivated adults in the proper sense of the term; we are even unable, to take an even more banal example, to send them to bed at a sensible time, to get them to obey us without arguing pointlessly, without negotiating, when we know full well that they risk being dead beat the next day and unable to concentrate in class. We love our children so much, *we love them, if truth be told, sometimes so badly and we also want so much to be loved by them* that we lack that minimum of authority without which it becomes difficult to bring them up, and even more difficult to educate them.

Love is the problem but it is also the solution

Love plays tricks on us. It undermines authority and our capacity for work. Here too, although it can cause problems, it's a source of solutions: I'm convinced that it's not by putting the clock back, by any 'restoration' in the political sense of the term, any stepping backwards in the name of some hardline 'republican' stoicism, that we are going to overcome these problems today. *On the contrary: it is thanks to love for our children that we will finally realize that we also need to hand on to them Law and knowledge, that a moment of authority, effort and work is necessary to their future quest for a good life.* Truly loving them, loving them 'well', means becoming aware that in their own interests, the moment of authority and work is vital for them.

Claude Capelier: This triptych, Christian, Jewish and Greek – love, Law and works – is present throughout the history of Europe but in different proportions, depending on principles that change from one period to another. If these days Law and works have taken a bit of a knock, thanks to the revolution of love, it's not just by simply demanding that the balance between them be restored that it will all come right. Love has its own dynamic and, since it has become the foundation of our way of apprehending life, it's only on the basis of what it treats as of value that we can hope to rebuild a fruitful connection with Law and works ...

Luc Ferry: And that's exactly how love, as often, can as it were 'correct itself'. You're right to say that this triptych has always existed: upbringing has probably always been based on love, Law and works. However, these days the proportions are not at all the same, just as the nature of law itself has changed. To take one concrete example, the figure of the 'maternal father' didn't exist in my childhood. Fathers would allow a child to enter their field of vision only when it was five or six, not really before. The infant was much more its mother's than the father's child. Today, the two roles, maternal and paternal, are drawing ever closer. Of course, we can always qualify this and come up with counter-examples, but the overall observation remains true. Feminists will point out, correctly, that mothers continue to take on the larger share of housework and are usually more proactive than are fathers in organizing their children's school lives or leisure activities. The fact remains that in fifty years, whatever one says, the way fathers and mothers have started to come together and share the upbring- ing of their children has probably made more headway than in five hundred years! We've all changed nappies and bottle-fed our babies, in a degree to which our grandfathers were almost com- pletely unaccustomed.

The first thing which we need to take care of, however humdrum this may seem, is that children are sufficiently 'well brought up', as traditional families aptly put it, so that, when they start school, they're in a fit state to learn what they are taught without their teachers being reduced to doing the work that the parents have neglected. We are living through a period when we 'chuck all the problems into school', like chucking everything down the drain. We rely on it more and more since we haven't managed to build up authority within the family.

This confusion in respective roles also produces nefarious results in two ways. I wouldn't want teachers to get involved in the upbringing of my children, not just because this isn't their proper job but because I also don't think that it's desirable as such: upbringing is part of the private sphere and belongs in the family. Of course, it would be dangerous to try and establish an absolutely watertight division between what comprises upbringing and what belongs to education; there's always an overlap between them. Just as it is annoying to see parents endlessly disputing the authority of teachers and their legitimate pedagogic aims, the latter must likewise keep any initiative they take in upbringing within the limits of the most elementary rules of common morality and the principles of secularism: this was already what Jules Ferry required in his famous *Letter to Schoolchildren*. A teacher isn't there to give an opinion about happiness or the good life, any more than about politics or religion. So it's essentially a matter of upbringing being given within the family before the child starts school, and in a more complete form before starting primary school. Thus we parents need to ensure that authority is imposed, which doesn't mean we need to put on a display of authoritarianism, but that we need to be able to give children a sense for the Law for effort and work.

Let me make myself clear: I'm not arguing for a 'return of authority' in traditional guise. I'm convinced that, within the new framework of the modern family, we can invent other forms of authority compatible with the primacy of love, which requires the prior application of a perfectly simple principle: we need to pay special attention, in bringing up our children, to what seems in our view to deserve saying firmly 'no' and what justifies our unhesitatingly saying 'yes'. We need to ensure that what we approve of and what we forbid are motivated by reasons consistent enough for us to stick to them without this little shadow of doubt that always undermines authority and which can be perceived by our children – who then become past masters at taking advantage of it and starting to bargain. This is the first condition for our 'yes' to mean 'yes' and our 'no' to mean 'no' – in other words, for there to be no negotiation with children, or at least no interminable negotiation. Here again, I'm not saying we shouldn't ever argue with our children, but that negotiation must be kept to an absolute minimum.

All this is so commonplace that it might be found a bit silly: but I think it touches on some of the very profoundest issues. If the absence of law is damaging, 'authority for authority's sake' produces dismal effects. Many parents don't arrange the things they forbid into any kind of hierarchy, so they often put arbitrary, whimsical or pointless refusals on the same level as the most essential demands. You don't forbid a child of three from nibbling at a piece of paper, which has never killed anyone, in a tone of voice comparable to the one you'd use to stop it from scratching a baby or calling its parents idiots. It's crucial to be able to indicate that certain demands have a non-negotiable importance, while others are merely circumstantial or of limited extent: in this way, children will be gradually able to internalize a proper scale of values. All too often I see parents saying 'no' to certain requests quite arbitrarily, and thus (of course) without any real conviction, when they might quite harmlessly say 'yes', just because they're afraid of not having enough authority. It also happens that they are so scared a child might hurt itself that they end up forbidding each and every little thing as if it were a crime.

I'm sorry for bringing in these rather trivial examples but it's to show that, when it comes to authority, we need ourselves to be sufficiently sure of our ground for the child to realize that 'no' really does mean 'no'. The child needs the serene and thoughtful authority of the Law to build up a personality, to enter, as Lacan says, the world of the symbolic, the public space, the world of civility. This upbringing should be given to the child before it enters the world of school since, as I've said, it's not the teacher's business to assume this task.

Claude Capelier: Putting the way one demands or forbids different things into some sort of 'hierarchy' as you say is, these days, in most families, based directly on love. This profoundly alters our ideas about what is called the way we say 'yes' or 'no'. To begin with, we wish to limit the things we forbid to the really important matters. Then we tend to shape our expression of these prohibitions to suit personalities – our children's, first and foremost, but also our own. Then we pay attention, in our children, to feelings, likes and dislikes, anxieties and ideas that are much more varied than they were in the past: this too changes to some extent the range of the things we forbid and the way we explain them. We wish to give the people we love possibilities for maximum fulfilment, to have the most positive relations with other people of which they are capable, and, on the basis of these considerations, we define the rules and prohibitions we are not going to give way on since we realize that they're the necessary condition for fully human and civil relationships. This is very different from the old attitude which, all too often, consisted in imposing authority simply because it was in line with tradition or with some generally accepted maxim. Even when the Law we impose is quite simply that of common morality – and this is just an inevitable part of *upbringing* – *we* add 'overtones' or extras that stem from the variety of the feelings I've just mentioned. When love is the principle, the interplay of activity and prohibition is focused on the child itself and on our relation with that child. But this doesn't stop us – quite the opposite – fixing a certain number of guidelines for the reasons we've been discussing.

Luc Ferry: You're quite right. The basic principle of upbringing in the future is this: it is out of love, and not through some return to traditional forms of authority, that we – however much we may be parents of today, 'modern' parents – realize that authority, and thus the Law too and the work necessary if they are to acquire knowledge, are vital for our children. This isn't, as I've said, a way of 'turning back the clock': that's where our neo-Republicans are wrong. It's not a return to the Third Republic, to a 'harsh upbringing', a mainly authoritarian conception of the parents' role. It's really out of love that I realize that it's vital for my children to enter the space of the Law, of knowledge and of great works – just as vital as clothing them or housing them decently ...

I've always been exasperated by those parents who, as in traditional families, still spend a whole afternoon trying to force their child to finish the plate of spinach that makes it want to throw up. I've never inflicted this on my daughters. I absolutely fail to see why we impose on children what we'd never impose on ourselves. One of my great joys, once I was an adult, was telling myself that never again would anyone force me to swallow leek soup, that bloody soup which ruined my life when I was three or four! Parents think they're doing the right thing, I know. They want their children to have a 'balanced' diet – a dreadful phrase that I still can't hear without an ironic smile. So they need vegetables, especially greens, but – as everyone knows – the children who like them are very few and far between. They prefer pasta with plenty of butter, or rice, or even, *horresco referens*, a horrible (but divine) McDonald's! What are we supposed to do? I'm not saying we shouldn't seek to get them to eat a 'balanced' diet, or even ask them to make an effort occasionally but, please, let's avoid those high dramas that can spoil entire Sundays!

What I mean by giving this example – which quite a few people will recognize, I think – is that if I can judge from the time and the grim determination that some people devote to it, all the priorities of a sensible upbringing are turned upside down when we end up turning the consumption of carrots or leeks into one of life's big issues! It's as if eating leeks were as important as listening to Mozart, finishing your French homework or understanding binomial expansions in maths! This is an excellent illustration of the fact that we too often say 'no' for no real reason and that we force our children to make an effort in areas that really don't deserve it.

On the other hand, it's entirely beyond me how parents can be so stupid and thoughtless as to let their children kick up a hell of a racket on a beach or at a restaurant, a place where we're in a space of civility. This is barely tolerable and it doesn't bode well for their schooling, where you can be sure that a lack of respect for others will manifest itself towards the teachers as well as other pupils. It's this lack of upbringing in civility that ruins teachers' lives and stops them giving their lessons in the proper conditions; this is what created a permanent background noise in the class since the children just natter away and never stop fidgeting, as they're unable to concentrate. This is something more worth trying to get right than the 'noble cause' of forcing them to eat up their greens! Here it really is worth saying 'no', getting the child to realize that it's non-negotiable.

As a guideline in these questions, the principle of love is excellent. As I've said, we just need to think about what we really want, on the basis of the love we have for our children. This is the minimalist adage of love: 'Don't do to others what you wouldn't like to be done to you.' This training in effort, civility, listening to others, this training in calmness, hard work, concentration, is part of bringing children up and it needs, if I may say it again, to be sorted out before children start school.

The revolution of love has considerably enriched and diversified our relationships with our children, and this has opened the way we bring them up to new dimensions of human being

Claude Capelier: We've been talking a lot about rules of life and prohibitions, but in my view it's obvious that, in the way we bring up children these days, many other things have changed in directions that involve not so much the limits we impose on them but the positive development of their potential and their talents. This is clear, for example, in the wider range of subjects we can discuss with them, in the fact that we are bothered to follow their arguments and sound them out as much, if not more, than we would with an adult, even if (of course) in different forms. But it is also clear in the way we treat them as precious and in the variety of experiences we endeavour to give them.

Luc Ferry: Yes, it's true; up until now I've been treating upbringing as a preliminary to education, in other words, what parents ought to do so that the upbringing children receive within their families can enable teachers in schools to teach them without any difficulty. This is why I have initially tackled the question of upbringing, if not negatively, at least mainly from the point of view of authority, of prohibition – in short, of the Law. But it is self-evident that, in our relations with our children, we are these days developing many other dimensions.

And this is vital, especially as we live in a world that is almost entirely given over to consumption, a world in which there is a constant temptation to buy hundreds of things. Indeed, our societies have become societies of hyper-consumption. So there is a real risk of our children becoming constantly tempted, irrespective of the love we may show them, irrespective of the question of authority or Law, by the argument that Lucretius had already suggested was dangerous, at a time when it hadn't yet become the common rule: that of the boundless desire for novelties, a desire which gives you ephemeral joys accompanied by repeated disappointments, a sort of 'deceptive thrill', or even an addictive buzz, that leads people to consume and re-consume, over and over again, in a restless pursuit. At Christmas, our children are literally stuffed full of toys of which a considerable number will be found a week later in some corner of the room, already broken or abandoned.

Here, too, I don't believe in breaking away from this logic in some brutal, authoritarian way – even if it is pretty dismal: this would be possible only if we radically cut our children off from the world in which they are called to live, and confine them within the narrow circle of a family living artificially within itself, on the margins of contemporary life. It is difficult to imagine a worse way of preparing them to be autonomous and to feel comfortable in a society where, on this hypothesis, they would know nothing or would hate everything. We need other means of helping them to acquire guidelines and above all to develop a richer inner life that will mean they don't just suffer passively the pressure of fashion and don't succumb to consumerist addiction but can strike out on a path less dependent on material seductions.

So, if we are to raise them above the sphere of mere consumption, we need to inculcate in them the feeling that, as Pascal says, there are 'orders of reality' and that they are not all equally valuable. Buying things is enjoyable, of course, but we need as it were to prove to them, in our deeds and not just our words, that they can do better. I realize that this is very difficult at present. To give another concrete example, we can tell them stories – if possible, wonderful stories, for instance the great Greek myths, when they're young. We need to talk to them, as Bettelheim recommends in his fine book on fairy tales, about everything, including the coarse stuff, mentioned in these stories, without being afraid of going into details – so long as we do this as part of the ordinary conversation and don't relapse into pedagogic gravity. We need to give them the dimension of culture that is – forgive me for saying so – as often as not the complete converse of what is usually understood by the word 'culture' in TV programmes. Culture, true culture, is in my view neither the culture industry [*l'industrie culturelle*], for example the pop song, nor the avant-garde of the kind you find in FIAC, the international contemporary art fair, or Monumenta ... Indeed, it's the opposite, and it's not so difficult to identify this 'opposite': when works of art have survived for centuries, when they are still being taught, as is the case with fairy tales and Greek myths, in every university in the world, it's highly probable that there's a reason for this! Let's start with the classics, it will always be time to look at the pop song or the avant-garde a bit later ...

Let's spend half an hour every evening, or even just a quarter of an hour, reading the great fairy tales to our children when they're very young or, a bit later, the Greek myths, and then the great works of literature. We'll be presenting them with a marvellous gift, creating a personal bond with them and giving them cultural points of reference without even having to think about it – but these things are also a wonderful 'transitional object', a fine subject for discussion and a way of sharing ideas, values and feelings. In short, it's a magnificent way of bringing love into existence, making it individual, varying it and 'schematizing' it as one might say, using the philosophical term.

In connection with this, I've written a book on Greek mythology in which I tell the original versions of the great myths (and not the watered-down, deformed and often emasculated versions found in children's anthologies) so that parents can tell the stories to their children. I wrote this book with two thoughts in mind.

The first was that the great Greek myths speak of everything that children, and adults too, find fascinating: death, sex, love, war, our relationship to the cosmos, salvation, honour, fame, extraordinary adventures, crime and punishment, fate, and so on.

All human life is there. These stories are full of suspense: adults can share their children's excitement – but they are also wonderful topics of conversation. Now love can give rise to really interesting relationships only if it takes the form of particular conversations, singular relationships, everyday exchanges. When we read these stories and take part in the discussions to which they give rise, culture appears as a transitional object between people who love each other. Thus it becomes more interesting – and, if we go about it the right way, it can even at least partly compete with the world of consumption and TV.

And this brings me to my second idea, namely, that we need to show our children very early on that there are, as I said, orders of reality, that there is something higher than consumption. Our children should share the feeling we've all known as adults when we've just finished a book we've really enjoyed and now want to read the sequel. We'll never escape from the logic of pure consumption, which can become harmful, unless we find some way of containing it and going beyond it. In my view, it's the imperialist logic of consumption that we need to oppose. And we won't free our children from it just by depriving them of TV, computers and video games.

I explained just now why this, in my opinion, would be counter-productive. I'm more susceptible to the logic of the pastry baker who tells his apprentices: 'Eat all the chocolate éclairs, all the cream puffs, all the titbits you like. Within three months they'll be coming out of your ears; you'll want something else.' Of course, we need actually to take our children somewhere else, give them the idea that there's something that goes beyond the world of consumption. We don't need to deprive them of this but to lead them towards a higher world. This world is the world of culture understood not as a product of consumption or of constant innovation, but as a place of great works of art in so far as this place is above the world of consumption.

Claude Capelier: Your analysis could be applied more widely. Like you, I believe that the great myths and masterpieces provide us with irreplaceable cultural pointers through the emotions they give us. This is because they develop possible forms of a really deep and powerful relation to existence, and these enable us to find our bearings in life in a freer and more informed way. But in the families that, for whatever reason, remain deprived of the culture of the book, we can find, when they are loving and attentive, an equivalent for what you're describing. They use stories about (or told by) grandma, an uncle, friends and neighbours, in connection with films or TV soaps, to weave conversations in which adults and children swap ideas, forging richer and more substantial representations, in an often emotion-laden and tender environment. While high culture has an irreplaceable role, what I'm referring to shows that, in the modern family centred on love, relations with children have become considerably broader and deeper in even more varying ways than what we have so far discussed.

Luc Ferry: When I was talking about fairy tales or Greek myths, I wasn't talking about 'bourgeois' or 'refined' culture, but about popular culture. What counts is the 'transitional' character of works, ultimately works of any kind: I mean the fact that they act as a moral, emotional and intellectual mediation with our children. And it is probably this which has most changed with the emergence of the modern family – and we need to make the most of it, more than we are probably doing at present.

Previously – and this goes for peasant, bourgeois or aristocratic families – a child didn't say anything much at the table. If he wanted to say something, he had to ask for permission in an almost ceremonious way – and his request was often met with a refusal. Silence was the rule: children didn't speak. People ate in silence. The well-known horror of Sunday, symbolized by the family 'Sunday lunch', is largely connected with what I'm saying here. Things have changed, sometimes radically, and here too we need to make the most of this. Lunch is no longer an interminable ceremony where children listen in silence to their parents chewing, but it may be – if, of course, we don't use the occasion to 'get it over with' at a corner of the table with ready meals – one of the best opportunities to establish links between the generations. When we have friends round, we tend increasingly to place the children at the same table as the adults, with the intention of enriching their minds, and we no longer ask them to keep quiet.

Love needs mediation. In this connection, I remember a book – *Belle du Seigneur* – that provoked some controversy among young philosophers, especially at informal evening meetings organized by my old friend Castoriadis. It was a cult book and was endlessly debated among us. In this fine book by Albert Cohen, there's a passage, if I remember, where Ariane and Solal, the two main characters, who are madly in love with one another, withdraw to a hotel. Here they are alone, face to face, in what is really a duel from which the others and the rest of society are excluded. They very quickly start looking daggers at each other and realize that being head over heels in love like this, when deprived of any social mediation, just goes round and round, turns sterile, not to say destructive. They've whispered countless sweet little nothings to one another, they've kissed, made love, they've told each other how adorable they both are, but they end up feeling bored to death. Why? Because they come up against a need for mediation, for society, for some third term, for what I called a transitional object if their love is to find some concrete shape and not wither away.

This is exactly what we experience with our friends, our wives or husbands, our mistresses or lovers, but with children too: we need mediation, transitional objects on the basis of which our love can be varied, become more particular and concrete – I'm using several terms since I can't find any more suitable word outside the jargon of philosophy (where 'schematism' covers it). We can't spend all our time telling each other 'I love you', 'you're such a darling', kissing our children on the cheek ... We need to 'articulate' love. I've chosen Greek mythology, not out of any 'bourgeois' mindset, not so that my children will have a 'refined' classical culture – even though there's nothing so wrong with that! – but above all because these great myths are brilliant from the literary, psychological and metaphysical points of view because they touch, as I've said, on all the great subjects. They enable us to have with our children, if not adult conversations, at least conversations on adult subjects and with far fewer taboos than was the case in the past.

It was with this in mind that I also mentioned Bruno Bettelheim's book on fairy tales. I find it quite admirable. In it, Bettelheim explains for instance why it is wrong to present children with watered-down versions of the tales, in which the most 'shocking' scenes are censored or euphemized so as not to 'traumatize' children and to bring the story more in line with morality. In the original fairy tale of *Snow White*, for instance, in the version by the Brothers Grimm, the stepmother has to put on white-hot iron shoes and dance until she falls dead. In *Cinderella*, the two sisters cut their feet off so they'll fit into the 'glass' slipper.[1] In these original versions, the description of sadistic details, of the harshest punishments, and even of aspects of romance and sexuality enables children to free what lies within them and to seek in fiction ways of answering their most secret ponderings: the fact that adults aren't forbidding them to think about such things, since they're ready to read these stories out to them and talk about them together, relieves them of guilt. It's terribly emancipating and can give rise to discussions that are sometimes marvellous or enchanting. This is all part of the loving relationship we have with our children, one that's so much finer and deeper than the limited relation, full of prohibitions and censorship, that adults all too often had with their equivalents in the traditional family some fifty or so years ago.

The fact remains that this new freedom of lifestyle shouldn't result in children starting school without picking up the behaviour, the attitude and the discipline necessary for their lessons to be of use to them and to be given in the right conditions. This remark naturally leads us to the second element in this part of our discussion: education in the age of the revolution of love.

Education nowadays has to face three new difficulties

I will be focusing, right from the start, on three relatively unprecedented problems – or problems that are at least new if we compare today with the 1950s when people thought they had been, or at least were being, sorted. These are three problems which education comes up against these days, and nobody in good faith can argue that they don't exist. The modern family, as I've said, is not all good news and, if we are to get the best out of it, it is in our interests not to be blind to its drawbacks.

---

[1] In the best-known French version of the legend, that by Perrault, the slipper is made of *verre*, meaning 'glass'. The slipper is also of glass in other versions, such as the English one. But it has sometimes been surmised that the French *verre* at some stage homophonically replaced *vair*, i.e., squirrel fur, a more plausible though less poetic material for a slipper.

The rise in illiteracy

First, there is the huge issue of illiteracy. The struggle against this tragedy was our hobby-horse when you and I were both working in the French Ministry for Education between 2002 and 2004. Before commenting on the alarming, convergent and, unfortunately, now perfectly well-established statistics, I'll just set the ball rolling by mentioning one particularly suggestive survey carried out by the Direction des études et statistiques, the statistical office of the Education Ministry in the mid-1990s: it was based on copies of school certificates from the 1920s that had been forgotten and then discovered in an attic in a sub-prefecture of the Somme – 9,000 copies of school certificates, in other words, a representative sample that meant performances could be compared, especially in proficiency in the French language, with those of pupils today. The director of this department carrying out the survey took care to eliminate any bias, anything that might invalidate the comparison. As we know, the teachers entered only 10 or 12 per cent of their pupils for this school certificate and they spent the whole year preparing them for it: so it was decided to compare them with a 1995 panel of good pupils in the *cinquième*.[2] Of course, all the subjects no longer studied were omitted. They also made allowances for the fact that France was then much more rural than today: so a new criterion for selection was added to ensure that the sample of our *cinquième* pupils would have the same sociological composition as the group that took the exam in the 1920s.

In spite of all this, the results of the survey, especially in proficiency in French language, were catastrophic for today's pupils (see *Les Dossiers d'Éducation et Formation* no. 62, published by the Ministère de l'Éducation nationale, February 1996). In the dictation exercise, we now find an average of seventeen mistakes, as against five in the 1920s. The survey was, as I said, carried out in 1995. Today, the results would be much worse as the situation has deteriorated considerably.

With my friend Admiral Bérau, I produced a study that combined the different figures from the Education Ministry with those of the Defence Ministry (see Luc Ferry et al., *Combattre l'illettrisme* [*The Fight against Illiteracy*], 2009). These figures are of great

---

[2] The *cinquième* is the second class in secondary school.

interest, since during the Journées d'appel et de préparation à la défense (JAPD, now the JDC),[3] eighteen-year-olds take 'life-size' tests: this is no longer a 'representative sample', a comparison between samples, but the real life situation of a single cohort. What we find, when we combine the data gathered by both ministries, is that between 30 and 35 per cent of our children, from the start of secondary school up to school-leaving age (the figures are unfortunately the same), are on average experiencing great difficulties in reading and writing. Of them, between 7 and 8 per cent are completely illiterate, between 10 and 15 per cent are very poor readers, and 10 per cent can read all right but only very slowly, which means they can't read for pleasure and have encountered difficulties in their studies.

150,000 young people emerge from the school system each year practically without any certificates or qualifications

Then we come up against a no less dramatic problem: around 150,000 young people emerge from the school system each year practically without any certificates or qualifications. For a tiny number of them, they have a school *brevet* or the equivalent, as people say in professional channels, but such tests do not correspond to any officially recognized diploma.[4] So all these young people are emerging from the educational system as real school failures.

Over 80,000 'serious incidents' per year are reported in educational establishments

Finally, we also find between 80,000 and 90,000 serious incidents – really disturbing things: violence, drug trafficking, weapons trafficking, sexual attacks, and so on – are noted each year in our schools. And we need to add that this is just the tip of the iceberg

---

[3] JDC = Journée défense et citoyenneté: like the JAPD, which it replaced in 2010, this is a day designed to give young French people (of both sexes) an insight into careers associated with the military; it is meant as a partial replacement for national service and involves testing the reading level of the candidates.

[4] In this context, a *brevet* is a relatively modest diploma; the *diplôme national du brevet*, for example, is a general qualification generally obtained between the ages of 14 and 16.

since this includes only the most serious incidents reported by head teachers who, of course, don't report everything.

So, in summary, what we have here are three major problems. The first is an enormous rise in illiteracy. If I'd told my grandmother, who was a head teacher, that the main problem in French schools in the 2000s would be illiteracy, she would have fallen off her chair; for her, this problem had already been sorted, at least for all the pupils who went to school assiduously, as the law made it compulsory after Jules Ferry. The second problem is the breakdown in civility, the violence – in short, the crisis of authority. This coincides with the massive failure comprised by those 150,000 young people who emerge from the system far below the level of the baccalaureate, which is not enough for them to find their way in life or to have any real professional qualification.

What lies behind these recent failures, if not on the part of the schools, at least on the part of schoolchildren?

Why have things regressed so much? Most of the time, especially in neo-Republican circles, the blame is unthinkingly laid at the door of the 'school system', as if this were quite self-evident. I think this is largely wrong: the truth of the matter is that the school system has not changed much. It might indeed be criticized for this. In any case, it's no worse than it was. The recruitment of teachers is more exigent than ever, especially those who teach in secondary schools. The competitive exams are extremely difficult: teachers are recruited at the level of a Master's when, in the 1950s, 1960s and even 1970s, they were recruited at the level of the baccalaureate and even the BEPC.[5] Given this, blaming the school system or the quality of the teachers is in my view as pointless as accusing the 'global method', another windmill at which old-school Don Quixotes like to tilt, when this method disappeared almost a quarter of a century ago from almost all the classes in which pupils were taught how to read. Decrying pedagogic

---

[5] *Brevet d'études du premier cycle*, awarded to pupils at the end of their fourth year in secondary school.

syllabuses, theories and practices is also a *pons asinorum*, a ritual that soon becomes facile. The fact of the matter is this: *it's society as a whole that is in a bad way, rather than teachers or the 'system' – as I've said, the latter are, if anything, better than in the 1950s. It's the pupils who have become difficult because they haven't been given, by their families, an upbringing that really prepares them to receive an education worthy of the name.*

What I'm saying is said by nobody, or almost nobody, else, and I know that I'll shock some readers who will conclude that I'm seeking to take the responsibility away from the Ministry of Education. But far from it: indeed, I'll shortly be turning to its tasks, to what it can and must do. But it's always easy to take glib pot-shots at the teachers, the 'system', the administration, the minister, rather than cleaning up one's own backyard and thinking about the family. This doesn't mean that the minister is unable to do anything – I'll be coming back to this, too – but that, for lack of upbringing, education becomes quite simply impossible.

Admittedly, on the pedagogic level, three major mistakes have been made over the last forty years. And these mistakes are, as I'm about to spell out, those of society in its most fundamental tendencies. In fact, they are *paradoxically the perverse effects of the inflation of the feelings we have for our children.* And, here again, we see that the rise in the intensity of love and emotional bonds in families is not entirely an unmixed blessing.

What are these mistakes?

'No old folks, no masters'[6]: the 'cult of youth' as a counter-culture that turns school culture into something outmoded

The first mistake is a kind of crazy cult of youth that is dominating our societies in ever-more obsessive ways. Since the 1960s, youth has been endlessly overvalued, and people have not ceased to genuflect before what Louis Althusser called 'the continent of childhood'. Ever since then, they've become ever more Rousseauist, sometimes thoroughly demagogic, with the peak being reached in the 1970s. The first singer invited on prime-time TV explains how, in spite of being fifty, he's 'still young', how much he loves young

---

[6] '*Ni vieux, ni maîtres*': a variant on the anarchist slogan '*Ni Dieu ni maître*' ('neither God nor master').

people, is proud to work with them, to be loved and recognized by them, and even more, to be still one of them, in spite of a few white hairs ... 'I'm ten years old!': it's as if it were necessarily 'brill' to be ten, to have remained a kid, when in fact you're seventy ... This overvaluation of youth has of course been accompanied by a devaluation not just of old age, but more generally of adulthood. To become an adult is a synonym for catastrophe. I remember arguments with *soixante-huitards* who informed me that having a teacher holding forth in front of a class was a tragic and tyrannical mistake, and that children, even the youngest, had more to teach the teacher than vice versa – indeed (they said), the old folks should be tied up at the back of the class so they could finally give them a few life lessons!

This extolling of youth culture has had destructive effects, both on the general atmosphere of society and on the school system. Actually, teachers have dabbled in this ideology less than the rest: they were in a good position to see that it didn't have much to do with reality.

'I'm ten!' When I was minister for young people, I never stopped saying that you're not a great poet at the age of ten, nor a great philosopher, nor a great painter, a great composer, a great business leader, any more than you're a great pilot or a great footballer. At the age of ten, you're a young whippersnapper, maybe likeable enough or even loveable, but nothing exceptional. Anyone who wants to stay cooped up at the age of ten for ever is suffering from 'Peter Pan syndrome' as they call it, like the little boy who wanted to spend all his life in the world of Captain Hook, Wendy and Tinkerbell without ever needing to grow up – in other words, that crazy illusion which adults indulged in, quite dismally, in the 1970s: the illusion of the child who refuses to leave the world of the imaginary. But upbringing is simply the move from childhood to adulthood. *If we undervalued the point of arrival – adulthood – how could we have avoided also undervaluing the very process of upbringing?* Of course, as the saying has it, 'as you grow older, you just get stiff in different places', and it's not always pleasant to grow old. The fact remains that the world of adults – when it works out, of course – is more intense, richer, more exciting and more intelligent than the world of childhood. We need to show our children that it can be a wonderful opportunity to leave the world of Peter Pan.

The reign of the 'child as king' or the myth of self-constructing knowledge: a 'regency' in the name of which many mistakes ꜣꜣꜣ꜠ ꜣꜣꜣ ꜣꜣꜣ꜠

The second mistake, again linked to an over-'sentimental', not to say misguided love for children, is the advent of the 'child as king'. I don't like this phrase since criticizing it has become a 'right-wing' thing to do. More generally, among neo-Republicans, it's also a veritable *pons asinorum*. It might cause confusion among my readers. I don't intend here to put forward a particular 'reactionary' discourse. If I am still using this expression, it's because it's ended up becoming the standard formula for describing this phenomenon.

The cult of the child as king, which lies directly behind the excessive obsession with youth we've just been discussing, dominates upbringing but also a lot of education too, if not among teachers, at least among the 'supervisory' staff, in school syllabuses and the directives formulated between the 1970s and the 2000s: it's the basic foundation of the ideology of what has been called the 'renewal in pedagogy'.

It all began with the idea that education, as often as possible, if not always, ought to be based on active methods, on the child's 'self-construction' of knowledge. The child was then called upon to draw up the rules for the school, as if he were competent to do so and as if we adults were shrugging off the question of authority. All this with, between the lines, the illusion that children who have themselves drawn up the rules for their lives will better respect them – which is not a daft idea, but quite simply wrong. (This is not the same thing: a mistake, and this is the case here, can quite easily stem from ideas that seem perfectly rational.)

In the same spirit, the teacher's role as someone who stands in front of the class and talks was jettisoned in favour of pupils working on documents in history or science. Dictation was replaced by self-corrected dictation, formal essays by 'creative writing', extra emphasis was given to 'awakening the child's faculties' (which proved a complete failure), and so on. All these nice little ideas – which are far from silly but completely wrong-headed – are still doing the rounds these days in the ideology of 'hands-on' activity where pupils begin by cobbling things together, making miniature watermills to produce electricity, little steam machines to help them understand what pressure is, or the transformation of energy, and so on. All this is charming, a nice way of playing around – but it flies in the face of real work and also of what the teacher-directed lesson can produce with its remarkably high level of synthesis and concentration. In such exercises, the content is strung out for weeks on end: nobody realizes that the time wasted is not made up for by any higher quality in the knowledge accrued.

That fact of the matter is – and here we can see how much the road to hell is paved with good intentions – this God-awful 'renewal in pedagogy' sometimes rested on principles that were not necessarily stupid in themselves. It wasn't wrong, for example, to point out that the traditional hardline republican policy some-times looked more like a barracks than a school. There was some-thing quite relevant in the rehabilitation of the child, freed from a disciplinary school system. And the teacher standing in front of the class isn't the whole story: doubtless, some of his or her activi-ties must rest on the children 'self-constructing' their own knowl-edge. It's just that we've gone too far, overstretched ourselves yet again.

In the case of illiteracy, the figures speak for themselves: not only has the 'renewal in pedagogy' not eliminated failure, but, by reflecting the ultra-individualist aspirations of a part of civil society, it has helped to deepen that failure. With its hyperactive methods, its ideology of general self-construction, *its proponents have underestimated the fact that most knowledge, whether trans-mitted by upbringing or by education, stemmed (as I have stated elsewhere on several occasions) from tradition, in other words from the handing down of a heritage.* For this knowledge to be handed down, children as well as pupils need to show an attitude of respect and humility, not the arrogant omnipotence with which the child-king is endowed.

With regard to these mistakes, it is no coincidence that the two areas in which schools have most difficulty these days are illiteracy and a lack of civility – in other words, the two most traditionalist areas. None of us invented the French language; none of us invented the formulae of politeness or the rules of civility. In both these cases, we are involved with knowledge that is completely inherited, completely conventional and handed down by our parents and our teachers. But the cult of spontaneity, of creativity, of the active self-construction of knowledge on which so much emphasis has been placed over the past forty years, flies completely in the face of those traditional sectors of education: the mother tongue and civility. When I sign off a letter with 'Yours sincerely' or 'Yours faithfully', there's nothing in the least 'self-constructed', creative or spontaneous about the formulae: they are purely traditional. Likewise, all the spelling rules we learn in childhood – in English spelling, 'i before e, except after c', plural verbs with plural nouns, and so on – have nothing spontaneous or creative in them at all: they're just tradition and are mainly learnt 'by heart'. Of course, this 'by heart' can be more or less intelligent: we can give dictations that are assessed as a whole rather than dictations in which every mistake is penalized. The fact remains that it is vital to keep up a certain traditionalism in this area: to make myself perfectly clear, I'd say that creativity in spelling is wrong spelling. Creativity in grammar is bad grammar.

The mistake of the 'carrot-and-stick pedagogy': it's not motivation that precedes work, but the contrary – work precedes motivation

The third mistake, again connected with this sentimental regard for children, this constant way of wrapping them up in cotton wool, is what I call the 'the carrot-and-stick pedagogy'. This was, in my view, the biggest mistake made by 'pupil-centred' teachers. They were convinced that pupils absolutely needed to be motivated before they could be made to work. So teachers turned up with guitars, they played recordings of some trendy singer, they showed videos, they talked about feminine sexuality and about everything that was deemed likely to grab the attention of their pupils, everything that would boost what the Jesuits called the *captatio benevolentiae*. The problem is this: even with very appetizing carrots at the end of your stick, the pupil soon starts to get tired of a carrot-centred diet. For, conversely to what the 'pupil-centred' teachers thought, *it's not motivation or interest that need to precede work, but the opposite: it's work which, generally speaking, precedes interest.* We take a real interest only in what we have already worked on a great deal. A difficult discipline – philosophy, chemistry, history, geography or even music – becomes interesting only when we have practised it a great deal beforehand.

I'd add that I don't know of any means of getting my children to work without involving a moment of authority.

And, after all, what is a great teacher if not someone endowed with a personality that is not democratic but charismatic – someone who really stirs us to work and helps us get into works of art or gain access to difficult disciplines? This is probably because we don't want to seem completely stupid in the eyes of such teachers, or because they are full of charm, but also because they possess real authority and manage to make us work like crazy and thereby help us to understand that their discipline is, or at least may be, really exciting.

The kind of hyper-love or hyper-sensitivity that we have for our children has led us to forget all this. We feel so much love for them that we've tried to take all the bits out of their orange juice, remove anything boring from education, anything connected with *tripalium*. We've ended up losing on both counts: love hasn't gained anything and the authority of law and knowledge, those two such essential dimensions, have suffered considerably.

Should we motivate pupils with games or does hard work bring knowledge along in its wake?

Claude Capelier: I have to say that I don't agree with you when you say that work necessarily precedes interest in a particular discipline or work of art. As far as I'm concerned, at least, it was almost always because I was really excited by something – a question, a school subject, a work of art – that I started working on it like crazy. I also sometimes worked hard in areas that bored me but, with a few exceptions, they still made me yawn my head off just as much as before. It's precisely when I have a passionate desire to explain and master, as much as possible, the mystery that has dazzled me that I can quite cheerfully spend months doing some dry-as-dust, finicky piece of work so as to find out more about it or become capable of doing what I hadn't previously been able to do. As for charismatic teachers, who are the only ones who really count, I'm sure that it wasn't because I didn't want to 'seem completely stupid' that I worked on the subjects they taught but because they'd shown me the angle from which it all seemed exciting.

However, I share the main points in your analysis (we've discussed this many times), especially the fact that by emphasizing the 'self-construction' or the 'social construction' of knowledge, two fundamental things have been forgotten. First, with a method of that kind, we need five thousand years, in the best case scenario, to reconstruct our culture (and this is an unreasonable length of time to wait, given current human life expectancy). Second, a characteristic of human beings is to rely on the discoveries of their fellow humans to make their own; as Jerome Bruner has said (having failed to notice the fact for thirty years), 'culture shapes the mind'.

As for the 'carrot-and-stick pedagogy', I'd agree that, more often than not, it doesn't work, but in my view this is for another reason than the one you've just indicated. Most of the time, it consists in trying to draw the children's attention to something quite unrelated to the work they will be asked to do later on: they can't see the connection, and they're right. Conversely, a great teacher can show them something in music, literature or science that arouses their curiosity. One can then see that, if they work at it, their interest will increase. There's something much too simplistic in your way of putting it.

Luc Ferry: Well, okay, I too do not completely agree with what you've just said. But I think it may be, at least partly, due to a misunderstanding. Of course, the teacher has to show that he's not going to force us to work for hours and hours on subjects of no interest whatsoever. This is indeed a minimum requirement, and I can't imagine anyone disagreeing with that. But in spite of everything, there is in what you're saying a contradiction, an almost logical contradiction, pure and simple: how could a pupil, who is still by definition a child, take an initial interest in anything, a work of art or a discipline, of which that pupil is quite ignorant? And why should we eliminate the dimension of unexpected discovery that education may involve when we are tackling whole swathes of knowledge of which we had not the least prior idea?

When I discovered philosophy, by reading a piece by Kant that was on the syllabus for the baccalaureate, not only did I understand not the slightest thing about it, but I didn't even know what philosophy, that strange thing, was – it resembled neither literature nor science. Unless I'd had someone whom I trusted and could tell me I first needed to work hard, make an effort to read and understand, I don't know who would have made clear why it was worth reading the *Foundations of the Metaphysics of Morals*! And any attempt to make it clear would itself inevitably have been formal, abstract and thus without much interest ...

My point, then, is that we start to work, not because it's initially interesting – and you'd find it difficult to persuade me that philosophy is initially interesting – but because we trust an adult, in this case a teacher, and because we can see that the knowledge he or she has (and that we don't yet have) is an opportunity for attitudes or ways of talking that are captivating. And it's only much later, when we've really worked at it, enough to know our way around and understand things, that the work we're studying, which first repelled us, becomes interesting. And so I'd still say that, essentially, work obviously precedes interest.

From the point of view that you're putting forward, things are slanted because we start from something that children know already – for example, a song that they've heard and that they like – and go on, as good teachers, to show how it contains interesting features (harmony, rhythm, melody, whatever ...). When we're dealing with areas in which the child knows absolutely nothing, where he or she is starting from nothing, as is often the case, it's quite different. How can we get a child to understand from scratch the first book of Spinoza's *Ethics* or the beginning of Kant's *Critique of Pure Reason*? The first time we read it, all we can find to say about it is that, at first blush, it's gibberish! It's only when you see, in great teachers, like the ones I had – Heinz Wismann and Jacques Rivelaygue – that what they've learned for themselves, what is now literally part of them, enables them to speak with considerable eloquence, to say things of an intelligence and depth that I've never seen before or anywhere else – this gives you wings, a real desire to appropriate for yourself that rare and precious knowledge. And the only way to accomplish this is by hard work. And the bad teachers – and they exist too, unfortunately – are the ones who spoil their trade and can put you off a discipline or a work of art because they make you want to do anything except go and find out about it ...

Of course, I don't want to say the opposite to you: we do indeed need to give a foretaste of the interest that lies in some knowledge we are trying to communicate. I think we both agree on this. But it's one thing to say 'You'll see, it's really brilliant, trust me, just take a couple of hours and you'll see I'm not lying. I'm going to lift a corner of the veil so that you can see it', but it's something completely different to work at it properly. I didn't read Spinoza's *Ethics* or translate the *Critique of Practical Reason* for pleasure – I'd be lying if I said so. Work is more or less, and always will be, however exciting, a *tripalium*, a torture. There's a whole load of boredom, of pain, in work, and we put up with it only because we can foresee the importance of the subject. Nonetheless, we do foresee it, and this happens only after we've discovered it. It took me nearly ten years to grasp that Spinoza and Kant really were quite brilliant. When I was fifteen, I'd say to myself, 'I need to know this because there's obviously something grand in it all.' But I had absolutely no idea what they were on about. I'm sure that, deep down, we cannot fail to agree. The great mistake of education based on play, of using games to bring up children, of what I call 'carrot-and-stick pedagogy', is that it simultaneously underestimates the role of the teacher as 'seducer' and the place of effort and hard work.

Certain countries have found a solution to the 'breakdown of the school system': how?

Claude Capelier: You've placed your thoughts about what you call 'carrot-and-stick pedagogy' within a wider context of ideas about the set of causes that lie behind what Christian Forestier has called the 'syndrome of the breakdown of the school system'. The basis for these observations is the fact that, since 1994 precisely, all the statistical figures for the French education system are flashing red. And all countries in the OECD have experienced or are experiencing the same problem as us in education. What did, or do, these countries have in common? The desire – fostered by the reign of excessive love – to respect the diverse potentials of the child and of the teacher: for instance, this has led to many new points of view on what is involved in learning to read. In itself, this was quite progressive: an attempt was made to grasp the sociological, linguistic and even genetic aspects of learning to read. But it led to an unbelievable fragmentation in the activities supposed to help pupils master the written word. The result was that there was no

longer any continuity in the methods used. The aims, and the type
of exercises involved, changed radically from one class to another
and even in one and the same class. So parents no longer understood what was happening, the pupils could no longer distinguish
between the essential and the secondary, and the teachers themselves got lost in analytical schemes of ever-increasing complexity.
Over the years, any consistency ended up being lost. And yet
consistency is the first condition of all learning. Perhaps what had
been done in the fifties was pretty dumb, but at least it had the
merit of being continuous, which is not the case these days.

Now, a few countries have found a solution. They've chosen
methods that, at first blush, seem very different from one another
but, when we analyse them, we see that they have three points in
common that could act as guidelines for our own attempts to
imagine a solution that will work in France. To begin with, they
restored continuity in the teaching methods: either by resorting to
pragmatic means, as in Finland (where children are followed for
several years by the same team that is thus responsible for their
success), or else by a more hierarchical form of supervision, as in
South Korea. Then, they have ensured that teachers can help a
pupil who hasn't understood an exercise or a question 'in real
time', as soon as the problem arises, so as to stop difficulties
becoming constant irritations. Finally, they have made it a priority
to raise the level of all pupils to a maximum: the analysis of the
international PISA[7] survey clearly shows that systems that aim at
the success of all also create the highest-performing elites, while
the countries whose systems are more elitist widen the gap between
the less good and the best pupils, without managing to raise the
latter to the level of their peers in more egalitarian nations.

Luc Ferry: I agree with all that, of course. Nonetheless, the main
problem, if we try to summarize what we've been saying, is first
and foremost the devaluing of adult culture. These days, we find
ourselves in a kind of absurd configuration where adults and
young people are, on the cultural level, like two different tribes
that ethnologists have to analyse separately. In plain and simple
terms: old people listen to Mozart and young people to rap. It's
crazy. This devaluation of the adult world, linked to the cult of

---

[7] Programme for International Student Assessment.

youth, has been disastrous if you ask me, as has the decline in the capacity for work, so striking in the history of education. And here, too, if I may take up the thread of my argument, it's not so much the 'school system' that's responsible as society as a whole, whose failings it basically reflects, without always having the means to correct them, since upbringing flies in the face of education.

What initiatives should be most emphasized to overcome the current problems in schools?

Claude Capelier: Now that you've analysed the current problems in schools and the causes behind them, showing how they were connected with the revolution of love, it's time to indicate the directions that should in your view be emphasized to overcome them, if only in part.

Luc Ferry: The first idea I've put forward, though nobody has listened (*vox clamantis in deserto*) is this: children really have to learn to write, not 'before they start secondary school', but in the very first years of their junior schools, before they are seven or eight. Eighty per cent of children who don't learn to read in their first year of primary school never do so. So we need to pull out all the stops in the three years that run from nursery school to the end of the second year at primary, and divide into two (as I did for 75,000 pupils – a significant number) all the difficult classes, thus reducing to a tenth the number of children who are being taught to read in class. This concerns the classes situated in the places where the children are emerging from primary school with a failure rate of 50 per cent in reading and writing. So we need to divide the classes (and, as I've said, I did so, and it produced remarkable results, at least when the local authorities cooperated, which wasn't always the case) at the level of first primary year to ensure that a child doesn't leave this class, or at least the second year, without being able to read and write.

The idea that they ought to take an exam when they start secondary school is a bright one that doesn't work. This is for two reasons. First, it's much too late; the damage is done. We can't set up a barrier at entry level to secondary schools. And secondly, what are we going to do with those who don't get through? If it's a real exam, some of them are going to fail it. What shall we do with these pupils? Let's imagine they comprise just 10 per cent of a generation. What do we do with them after three years? After ten? Are there going to be hundreds of thousands of pupils kept on in the last year of primary school until the age of fifteen? An exam at entry to secondary school was meaningful only when there were extra classes, in other words, a vocational path set out for them as soon as they left primary school – and, I'm very glad to say, nobody wants this any more, not even managers. Those who failed the exam took the vocational route from the age of twelve. Who would dare to face children with such a dead end these days? Surely we're not going to turn out little workers who are school failures at the age of twelve? It's absurd. If we wish to remedy this situation, we clearly need to lay the emphasis on retaking the first year of primary, at the level of the cycle of basic instruction.

The second thing that needs to be done is to take spectacular measures to ensure that the vocational route is chosen for positive reasons, and not just as a second best: this means we have to extend it by excellent courses of such indisputable quality that they are internationally recognized. In other words, we immediately need to create four or five very fine schools, fine vocational *lycées*, the equivalents of Polytechnique, the École normale supérieure or Hautes études commerciales in the vocational sphere.[8] Of course, this needs to be done with the help of business and the sectors in which France is very competitive, such as pleasure boats, hotels, garments, computer software, and so on. We need to open vocational *lycées* that clearly and resolutely give access to every course, including at high levels, so that those who wish to and have enough talent can go as far as a vocational *licence*[9] or Master's.

Prior to that, it's urgently necessary to develop 'sandwich courses' that will allow children from the age of fourteen, when they so wish, to discover professions (I mean *discover* them, not practise then: I'm not talking about an apprenticeship), while

---

[8] Ferry is here referring to the elite, highly selective tertiary-level educational schools in France, the *Grandes Écoles*.

[9] The *licence* is the first university degree, very roughly equivalent to a Bachelor's.

following most of the general courses in the school: this leaves them with the possibility of then embarking on training that will prepare them for a profession which they can choose in an informed way or else go back to the general syllabus.

In conclusion, I'd like to say that, as opposed to what I so often hear, education isn't a lost cause. The worst is behind us. We've reached a time when it's possible to move beyond the slough of the barracks school and of 'pupil-centred teaching' alike. We're emerging from the difficulty – not (and this is where the neo-Republicans got it wrong) by retreating into the past, turning back the clocks, restoring the status quo, but for 'modern' reasons: the truth of the matter is that, out of love for their children, parents are really starting to realize that authority and knowledge need to be handed on too. This is rather a hopeful sign.

Art in the age of the second humanism

Claude Capelier: As we move from politics to education and, now, from education to art, we are gradually getting closer to the 'heart of the reactor', the place where the most intimate reactions fuse, as it were, with the most collective representations, the most common realities, so as to bring to light and develop, as Milan Kundera puts it, 'hitherto latent forms of existence'. We can observe 'from within', so to speak, the kind of transmutation through which love, the feeling – the most private feeling – par excellence – becomes the ultimate foundation of a vision of the world in which, consciously or unconsciously, we can all recognize ourselves.

It has often been claimed that artists of genius were 'in advance of their time'. I think there is some truth in this idea. It might be said, to cut a long story short, that the great painters of the Renaissance opened the way to a humanism that had to wait for Descartes, in the seventeenth century, before it could receive its philosophical foundation, and for the end of the eighteenth century to find a corresponding political realization in the shape of the French Revolution. It should be acknowledged that art has more immediate room for manoeuvre, with the painter's pigments, the musician's notes and the novelist's words, than does politics, where any new principle can be implemented only through a great variety of socio-economic processes, most of which resist it to a greater or lesser extent! As for philosophy, it necessarily comes on the scene only somewhat belatedly: we cannot think the present before it has manifested itself! This is the meaning of Hegel's celebrated aphorism: 'The owl of Minerva takes its flight only at nightfall.'

For all these reasons (and a few others that will appear later on), thinking about art, in particular about modern art and recent works, is a very good way of disclosing the early signs that suggest the paths that the revolution of love might take in the future.

Conversely, the analysis of works of art and of aesthetic experience gives us the key to a more subtle appreciation of our relationship to the world and to existence, now founded as it is on love: once this feeling becomes our guiding value and we desire to liberate all the fruitful dimensions of existence, we live our lives as if they were works of art being constantly created. We have entered an aesthetic age.

But the revolution in art goes beyond an aesthetic relation to the world because it provides us with a more general principle of meaning and engenders a new figure of the sacred, what you call 'the sacred with a human face'. The question is then that of knowing how modern art has contributed to this revolution, and how this revolution goes beyond it.

Modern art as an art of the deconstruction of traditions

Luc Ferry: Modern art and contemporary art are, first and foremost, arts of the deconstruction of traditions and of innovation, breaking away from the past and passionately seeking the new – and of course, if this were not so, it would be difficult to imagine why we call them 'modern'. Everyone will, I hope, agree with this without too much difficulty, but I prefer to begin straight away by focusing on some simple ideas, ideas on which we can agree, so as to highlight the points that are still controversial and, especially, the deeper lessons that can be drawn from them.

The famous exchange of letters between Kandinsky and Schoenberg at the start of the 1910s clearly brings out the extent to which their projects converged: they both explain in these letters that the deconstruction of figuration in painting corresponds perfectly with the deconstruction of tonality in music.

Kandinsky comes up with an extended metaphor which I find highly significant, one that can be found throughout the twentieth century: he compares cultural life, in this case artistic life, to a great triangle moving through time. At its peak we find genius. Kandinsky went on to suggest a historiography of modern genius that left its historical mark. In the field of the plastic arts, he says, it's Picasso who occupies the point that closes the triangle at its peak; in the field of music, it's Schoenberg. Just below this peak of genius, where there is room for only one person, we find those who are slightly lesser geniuses: in Kandinsky's view, these include Manet and Cézanne for the plastic arts, and Debussy for music. They are somewhat less audacious, somewhat less revolutionary, some less avant-garde. Then, the further we descend towards the base of the triangle, the closer we get to the 'ordinary doltish people', the 'stupid masses' who, by definition, understand nothing of the avant-garde.

Kandinsky then specifies what is perhaps the main feature in this mythology of the avant-garde: as the triangle as a whole moves up through time, one day or another the neglected geniuses (since they are in advance of their time, they are inevitably alone) will finally be recognized. Once the base of the triangle has joined the point where the peak of genius had been a few decades earlier, even the stupid mass of the populace, for which Kandinsky has nothing but sarcasm, will eventually acknowledge that those it had mocked or failed to recognize were indeed geniuses.

This image is quite clear. It underlines the extent to which the 'high' art [*l'art savant*] of the twentieth century emphasized an aesthetics of breaking away from tradition and permanently innovating, with both sides of the coin being inseparable.

In this connection, I also have in mind a short text by Duchamp that I quoted in *Homo aestheticus*: it's modestly called 'Apropos of Myself'. It's a lecture that he gave to an audience of Americans (who are naturally quite flummoxed), explaining to them that he changed style six times in a single year. This was his way of indicating the breadth of his genius. Not only was he innovative with regard to tradition, he was also innovative with regard to his own tradition! He was forever breaking away, not just from everything that had been done before him but also from what he himself had managed to do. In this, of course, he was suggesting to his audience that he was a pure genius. At the back of this ideology of the permanent clean break and continual innovation, we find a motif that characterized the twentieth century on every level: the deconstruction of everything that was part of a tradition.

In the field of art, people proceeded to deconstruct – this was the main theme of the Kandinsky/Schoenberg correspondence – not just tonality and figuration, but also the rules of classical drama with Beckett and Ionesco, of dancing with Béjart and Pina Bausch, of cinema with the New Wave (Godard, Truffaut and others), of the novel with the New Novel, and so on. All the traditional faces of culture were deconstructed one after the other.

And the end point today is that culture now has two faces that curiously enough are the only ones to be recognized by those who are oddly called 'opinion formers': on the one hand, the art of the avant-garde and, on the other, industrial culture. Boltanski at Monumenta, and the stars on the steps at the Cannes Film Festival ...

One 'deconstruction' can conceal another: behind the ideology of the avant-garde lies liberal globalization

The desire to break away on every level from tradition led most twentieth-century artists, with a few rare exceptions, to lay into bourgeois conformism, the mercantile economy, conventional taste and the gregarious illusions of the masses, in thrall to received ideas and advertising. Now this truth, although undeniable, conceals another, much more decisive and formidably paradoxical in appearance, even though it is obvious when you grasp its mechanism: behind this ideology of the avant-garde lay the rise of liberal globalization. I have developed this theme at length in my last few books, and so I won't go over it here: although avant-garde artists and 'bourgeois' industrialists despised one another for a long time (which is no longer the case, far from it, and we will be seeing why), capitalism and modern art nonetheless shared, each in its field, one and the same logic: that of permanent innovation and the destruction of the traditions necessary for it to impose itself. Marx was profoundly right: capitalism is permanent revolution.

For global capitalism to triumph, traditional values, in art as in lifestyle, had to be deconstructed by young people of somewhat revolutionary and utopian tastes, bohemians, doomed artists and unrecognized geniuses. After all, nothing hampers consumption so much as the possession of traditional values, as Marcuse had already noted in his phrase 'repressive desublimation'. For the ceaseless renewal of the values of fashion and consumption to triumph, to the greatest profit of the people launching new products, the traditional ideals of morality, patriotism and religion, but also conventions in taste, the old forms of representation, and so on, must no longer stand in their way, must surrender to them the main role in the structuring of individual and collective life. The dream of modern capitalism is this: modern consumers must not have in their minds any higher or even stable values that might prevent them from being endlessly haunted by the irrepressible desire to buy a new 'object of desire'. If our children had the values of our great-grandparents, they wouldn't buy three mobile phones per year or the equivalent in Nintendo games and so on. Before we could enter the era of addictive consumption, all the values tending to slow down mass consumption needed to disappear.

This logic, common to the artistic avant-garde and to capitalism, explains why the bourgeois and the bohemian, the 'doomed' avant-garde artist and the great captains of industry ended up being reconciled, at the end of the twentieth century, in the historic (I would even say 'historial' in Heidegger's sense) figure of what in French is called the *bobo*, the *bourgeois-bohème*, passionate about novelty, about creativity. The artist and the bourgeois now commune together in making sacred the third, common term: innovation. I would even say this is innovation for innovation's sake, now becoming a supreme principle, both for the bourgeois, capitalist and mercantile world – in which innovation is literally imposed by worldwide competition, by the absolute logic of benchmarking – and in the artistic world. When Jeff Koons and Damien Hirst, the two artists who are currently among the most well-known and most expensive in the world, bring out a new 'collection', so to speak, they have exactly the same strategies of communication, carry out the same manoeuvres and have the same ability to get enraptured people to share their vision, as Steve Jobs used to when presenting his new iPhone. What is being staged in both cases is this very logic of a break with tradition, this same permanent innovation.

Art is a market. Who is really interested in contemporary art these days? The big captains of industry, the big financial figures, the bankers – because they are all fascinated by innovation, which is their daily bread in general benchmarking. Ordinary people are light years away from contemporary art and, in any case, they don't have the means to bet on the art market.

It is no doubt exasperating for bohemians to have this convergence pointed out to them – especially to them, in fact, because they initially wanted to *épater le bourgeois*, maybe even swallow some worthy citizen every morning at breakfast. Ever since the *Petit Cénacle* of Nerval, Borel and Gautier, one of the first sites of the romantic, revolutionary and anti-bourgeois *bohème*, among the members of 'Jeune France' who were also called '*bousingots*' ['demagogues', 'agitators'] and would indulge in fisticuffs to defend Hugo against the 'old baldies' of the French Academy, this mythology of the avant-garde has been well established. Between 1830 and 1890, we can witness a sort of prehistory of modern art that seeks to be radically anti-bourgeois. This, perhaps, is the great paradox of the twentieth century: these days; not only has the *bohème* become bourgeois (in the sense that the great contemporary artists are incredibly wealthy, and their works are bought by the wealthy), but in addition the bourgeoisie have converted to the art of the bohemians, when fifty years ago they literally couldn't stand one another.

Claude Capelier: This is a theme on which you insist in several of your books, when you emphasize that the bohemians and the avant-garde artists unwittingly made life easy for global capitalism and, in this sense, they were 'the cuckolds of history'. But couldn't we look at things from the opposite angle? Great modern artists might well have taken deconstruction further and thus, in the face of the bourgeois who were scandalized by them, liberated forms of existence that had hitherto been undervalued or latent. But once these new dimensions of life had been brought to light and found valuable, in art and then in lifestyle, the very logic of capitalism maybe pushed our bourgeois business leaders to develop new products and types of marketing that responded to the emerging expectations that modernity had engendered. If what I'm saying is true, then this would qualify the idea that one group were the 'cuckolds' of the other. For on this hypothesis, it is indeed the avant-garde that discover new fields in which capitalists eventually catch up with them so as to capture new markets. 'One cuckold deserves another': if capitalists have profited from the 'deconstruction' of values, they have, at the same time, been obliged to follow modern artists on ground where, initially, they did not want at any price (quite literally) to set foot! In short, in my view the game is more equal than you claim; both groups seem to me to have profoundly modified the projects of their adversaries: the artists by managing to persuade the bourgeoisie to open up to something they found repellent; and the capitalists by profiting from what was supposed to bring them down.

Luc Ferry: In the final analysis, it doesn't really matter that it cuts both ways, which it probably does. What *does* count, however, is the way the logic of innovation for innovation's sake, the logic of making a clean break for the sake of it, was brought into the modern world in the twentieth century by means of capitalism and globalization: it was the latter which, by setting up fierce competition, open in every direction and on every level, ensures that innovation becomes the absolute rule governing the world. If you mean that deconstruction has liberated the world of desire and that a big capitalist can't fail to take an interest in this because it's the driving force behind consumption, well, yes, you're right. I think it's correct, but I don't think it's the essential point. In my view, this is tied up with two questions on which we need to linger for a while.

Beauty and innovation

The first is the question of knowing whether what interests us in art is first and foremost beauty or innovation ... or both of these. From my point of view, it's both. First of all comes beauty, of course. Otherwise, why take an interest in art, rather than science, philosophy or literature? Without a relationship to beauty, why, quite simply, should art exist? Of course, we also want innovations and an art that is of our time. There are probably composers alive today who would be technically able to write Beethoven's Tenth Symphony, but what would be the point?

Now if we lay the emphasis on beauty, most of contemporary art is extraordinarily unsatisfying. It's full of innovations of every kind, full of sometimes shocking or droll effects, but there's not much beauty in it. I recently had a surrealistic discussion with the teachers of a modern art school in Switzerland. When I addressed them – I was saying more or less the same as I am now – they told me, with some irritation, that they found *Fountain*, Duchamp's urinal, and the *Black Square* by Malevich extraordinarily beautiful.

I don't believe a word of it. It's pure snobbishness. And anyway, Malevich himself – you just have to read his writings – never claimed that he was in any sense aiming at beauty. When you read him, you realize that his celebrated square was just a way for him to deride what had been the model for perspective for centuries: the chequerboard for drafts or chess or the floor of Italian palaces that was used as models for teaching perspective and the vanishing point. He never claimed that *Black Square* was beautiful, any more than Duchamp claimed that the urinal put into the museum was beautiful. They merely felt like doing something absolutely new and subversive: the one because he was mocking traditional perspective; the other because he was destabilizing the pompous and unintellectual ceremony of museum exhibitions. As I said, this was never done, in any sense, with the aim of producing any beauty but so as to break away from tradition and create an effect of innovation. Likewise, there is no sense in saying that John Cage's concert of silence or the exhibitions without paintings of Yves Klein are beautiful. Here, we can see a chemically pure state of the break with tradition, innovation for innovation's sake pushed to its most radical term, not in beauty, not in any way ...

So my first point is this: if you're passionate about innovation, as is any self-respecting industrialist, then modern art and contemporary art may be brilliant; but if you're after beauty, there's precious little of this, in my view. If you're interested in both, as I am, you can find a few works that manage to reconcile them, but they are few and far between: Stravinsky or Bartók, for example, whose works are unarguably modern and sometimes have a beauty that takes your breath away. ... But not the black squares or the urinals nor any of the derivatives – like the heap of coal in the Bordeaux museum, or pianos set atop refrigerators in Darty, or a Simca 1000 abandoned in a barn and other platitudes of that ilk – that have been churned out in countless numbers over the last century and that are really produced by a conformist desire to provoke rather than by art ...

What should we do with the new dimensions of existence that modern art has liberated?

The second question that we need to discuss now, and we'll agree more easily on this, is one we've referred to several times here. It's the question of the liberation, through deconstruction, of dimensions of the human that had been hidden under the bushel by traditional art, even at its most grandiose, and *a fortiori* by all academicism. I know that this is what most interests you and basically justifies your love of contemporary art. And it's true: contemporary art and global capitalism will largely further the liberation which, as we've said, involves emancipating the unconscious, the body, sex, our animal side – but also the femininity of men, the masculinity of women, chaos, dissonance, the unrepresentable, the primitive, and so on. As Lyotard says, modern art aims to 'present the fact that there is something unpresentable'. Fine. It's all liberated: difference, otherness, the relation to the primitive, to other cultures, to childhood, 'intellectual realism', and so forth. In this way, dimensions of the human that nineteenth-century art did not take into account are liberated. As I've said, this is all true, I don't deny it, and it is, like all emancipations, in many respects a good thing.

The problem is knowing what we are going to do with the liberated material, so to speak. For if, in my view, Bartók and Stravinsky draw something brilliant from it in music, as do Kundera and Roth in literature, this is because they reintegrate the elements deconstructed and liberated by deconstructive modernity in musical form or in narratives that lead us, in contrast with the emotions and experiences they supply us with, to discover, in all their diversity, quite new variants of human being. In Kundera and Roth, there are characters, a plot, in short the staging of great human modern experiences: when you start reading their novels, you don't stop after thirty or so pages. Even so, these are not traditional novels: you avoid the terribly boring bits in the latter. I love Balzac but there are times when I have to admit I feel like skipping fifty pages or so. … Above all, these writers tell us about death, sex and love in a way these had never been described before. I recognize that it was probably necessary to take this detour through modern art and contemporary art to reach this point, to produce works that are both new and beautiful, thanks to the enrichment arising from what the deconstruction of the human had liberated.

Claude Capelier: Like you, I admire the composers and novelists you've just mentioned, but I'm not convinced by your completely reducing modern art to 'deconstruction' alone. I know that the philosophers of deconstruction analyse this particular point the same way as you do (and on more than one occasion!) but this isn't enough to persuade me to subscribe to your ideas. I'll happily grant you that there's always an element of deconstruction in an art that does indeed aim systematically at innovation, but I would claim that the greatest artists of the twentieth century were also *reconstructors*. Once a forgotten level of existence had been liberated, they devoted themselves to developing the world that was contained in it in a latent state, with the emotions, the poetry, the forms and the vision of the world that it secretly held within it. When Picasso paints a woman in her rocking chair in her kitchen and the walls are swaying, the colours are separated out and the lady's face twists and turns, I can see, I can finally sense the child-like beauty of those short moments we've always experienced and that, just as much as but more directly than a painting by Hooch, makes a world out of an impersonal moment in everyday life. In my view, we can't evade the task of shedding light on this question since it involves the very way that we may envisage the revolution of love: if it is true – as I believe – that the works of Joyce, of Klee, of Boulez and of a few others offer us worlds that give sensible shape to dimensions of existence that are emblematic of what we are living through at present, this changes the conception we have of the meaning of life to which the second humanism opens us.

I think that our difference of opinion stems from a confusion, and I recognize that this confusion is fostered by a certain number of artists who play around with past and present conceptions of art, by passing off a ready-made, for example, as the modern equivalent of a Rembrandt. If we wish to escape this confusion, I think we need to distinguish between three aspects of deconstruction.

The first consists in exploding the traditional connection people used to have with art and with the work of art. When Duchamp places a urinal or a bottle rack in the museum, we realize – this is the amusing side of it – that these objects bear a strange resemblance to a geometrical structure that might have been created by a contemporary artist. It's a way of cocking snooks at modern art, at the people who visit the museum and at the museum itself. It's a type of practical joke. Of course, nobody should see any beauty in this, even though it is being exhibited in a place that is supposed to be devoted to art.

Luc Ferry: I know you said you had 'three points' to make, but I'd like to intervene straight away on this one. It's not true that this misunderstanding has existed right from the start. In the prehistory of modern art, in the nineteenth century, in all those little bohemian groups (so delightful and charming), people were already inventing what Duchamp, Klein and Cage would do again later on: monochromes, concerts of silence, ready-mades. The difference between these first bohemian groups and contemporary art that becomes heavy and pompous is that *they* didn't take themselves seriously. They were creating something humorous whose philosophical role was to stand at odds with everyday middle-class life. When Alphonse Allais invented his work (and I find the idea behind it marvellous) *Aquarium in Frosted Glass for a Shy Fish*, after a few of his friends had dreamt up *See-saws on the Wall for Calming Unruly Children* or the *Comb for a Bald Man*, everyone realized that the aim was to break away from everyday life and the bourgeois world, but with humour and without pretentiousness. When, these days, we see Boltanski in the Monumenta exhibiting a crane with a five-fingered claw picking up rags, explaining mournfully that this is death striking at random, you have to pinch yourself to know whether you're having your leg pulled. This misunderstanding was not there at the start. After the 1900s, there was a time when this break with everyday life, which was humorous and joyful, became pompous and pretentious – and, what's more, it ended up being subsidized by the state, and even (this is really the limit) costing huge amounts of money, in an art market totally dominated by the logic of finance.

Claude Capelier: What you're saying doesn't contradict what I was describing. In Duchamp, there's a desire to foster this misunderstanding you've mentioned: he wanted to play, if I may put it like this, on 'every level at once'. What gave his gesture its impact was that he endeavoured to keep up the ambiguity to the very end, while the nineteenth-century bohemians dropped their masks as soon as other people laughed along with them. This said, once the procedure has been grasped, people aren't going to spend a hundred years contemplating a bottle rack. The effect is a short-term and rather basic one: this is a good example of deconstruction.

The second aspect of deconstruction is the procedure which consists of isolating an element of art or of daily life to bring out its unadorned effect. So it's not beauty which is being aimed at, but an effect. This can take very different forms linked, for example, to the spectacular magnification of the size of objects or the strange vibration of a colour, as in Klein's monochromes. Here too, however, I'm not going to spend hours in front of the painting. It was conceived in an elementary fashion, but the interest it arouses is equally elementary.

These two first tendencies are part of deconstruction, and I would be lying if I claimed that this were not characteristic of contemporary art.

But there is a third element, and I think it's here that we disagree. I'm convinced that a certain number of artists – you've mentioned some, such as Bartók and Stravinsky – have broken with tradition but also have the intention and sufficient genius to create a world. They are often extremely critical of the idea of beauty, in the sense that they don't want to follow the canons of traditional beauty, but they are evidently seeking to create a new form of it. This is the case with certain others whom you identify with the 'deconstructors' and who, as I've just said, strike me as marvellous 'constructors'.

When I heard Boulez's *Le Marteau sans maître* for the first time, I was struck by the music's beauty. If you listen to Boulez without any preconceptions, You can immediately note the ravishing quality of the sonorities: far from being the attack on our eardrums that many people describe, it's almost 'vampish', it's so full of velvet and gold. It's filled with instruments that use bells or pluck strings; there are incredibly rich sequences of chords – in short, the whole thing just sounds wonderful. It's not like tonal music, of course, but it sounds extraordinarily beautiful. If in nature you hear the sounds of waterfalls or bells chiming in the distance, you feel that it has a certain character and you find this immediate auditory charm in Boulez's music. It's another kind of beauty, which I was immediately seduced by. It swings, too, but with a unique variety – like a juggler catching balls in ever-changing circuits.

In particular, for the first time in my life, I was hearing a music that was developing with formidable inventiveness, creating the very effect of the relationship we have with the world and existence: different logics and universes that alternate and then are interwoven together, some moments that are clear and others that are enigmatic. It's like a maze and yet it's as obvious as a story experienced from within. Melodic effects (I sometimes sing them in the shower; I must be the only person crazy enough to do so) emerge from among elements that multiply, change and become locked in combat. It's an intensified recreation of the drama of life as I know it: you have very clear moments, moments when you don't really know where you're going and other, intermediary moments when you have several ways of interpreting things since you can choose to place the emphasis on one aspect rather than another, like when you're going for a walk through a forest. So in my view it creates a veritable universe.

When you listen to scenes from *Licht*, Stockhausen's opera, or even when you read the texts he wrote about it, you have to agree that his project is anything but deconstructive: he is trying to represent the totality of human life, as he himself says, and even of the cosmos beyond mankind. He is trying to find a music that will express this. Of course, this produces a world, and I don't think anyone can deny this.

Luc Ferry: Oh yes, they can! And if that produces a world, I'd rather live outside it. I've lost count of the number of times I've heard that *Marteau* you like so much, and I've just listened very intently to four of Boulez's other 'works', *Répons*, *Notations 11 'Scintillant'*, *Sur incises* and *Pli selon pli* (just from the titles, you'd think you were with Derrida at Yale, in the 1970s ...). When you describe them, it's magnificent, but when I listen to them, I can't hear any of what you find in them. I have the impression that's music written to a libretto by Derrida, in which 'dissonance' refers to *différance*. I know full well that, behind these compositions, there are tons of musical theory and sophisticated ideas, but it still doesn't work, at least not for me. Here, maybe, we come up against (and, after all, it's not so very serious) an essential characteristic of art, one of a doubtless terrible banality, but one you just can't get round: taste is and will always be subjective. Likewise, and I know I'm going to say something quite shocking here, and that I may even lose a few of my readers: I don't like, and I've never liked, Picasso. Houellebecq was completely right in my view to have been brave enough to say that Picasso has no sense of colour, that his paintings are dull and, in a nutshell, frankly awful. … I know he's a sacred cow – and I'm not! – but I don't know why it should be forbidden to say what we feel about art. And don't let anyone tell me, as always in these cases, that I don't 'understand' Picasso or Boulez. 'Understanding' has nothing to do with it – and anyhow, given the long time I've been working on, looking at, listening to and thinking about art, it's not the issue! On the other hand, we'll agree with one another more easily, for instance, about Kiefer.

Claude Capelier: I'm stupefied, to take another example from the field of literature, to hear you placing Joyce among the deconstructors when the whole project of his *Ulysses* corresponds in every detail with your revolution of love: by narrating in the form of an odyssey a single day, every episode of which brings out different dimensions of existence and their corresponding forms of expression, he is making daily life sacred through love.

The works I've just mentioned (I could have quoted many other examples – Klee, Kiefer, Faulkner, Duras, etc.) anticipate what you are describing in your philosophy of love: there is something more open about them and more loving than anything from before. Obviously, they are part of the modern movement of innovation and a break with the past, but their authors were geniuses, able to create a world.

Luc Ferry: If you can see in those great authors the same that I'm trying to think in my philosophy, I'm delighted and honoured, even though Joyce too bores me to death! What I find really brilliant in Kundera and Roth is that they are after all a real pleasure to read. However, they don't write airport novels. The difficulty of discussions of art is that they can't happen without an element of subjectivity that's their very essence. I can't argue on that level, I'm not going to say that you're wrong to like Boulez or that I'm right not to like him. The discussion here comes up against a limit and I can't see how, or even why, we need to go beyond it. We need to go further but on grounds that are no longer those of taste.

Claude Capelier: Exactly. You yourself acknowledge that certain authors in this trend have created a world. That's what's important. Some have managed to create a world in the contemporary context, in the context of deconstruction.

Luc Ferry: In spite of our shared goodwill, this is where we're not quite in agreement. When I take examples such as Stravinsky and Bartók, or Kundera and Roth, whom I really like, I don't think – far from it – that they belong to the movement of deconstruction. What is so brilliant in their work is just that they got out before the others: they are already 'post-deconstructionists'. In this sense, Stravinsky is much more 'modern' than Boulez. His music is beautiful, but not at all because it's 'still' rather traditional; on the contrary, it's because he went much further. That's real genius for you. I think that a certain number of very great artists and very great writers already invented a post-deconstructive world in the 1940s, 1950s or 1960s. In the plastic arts, I'd mention Francis Bacon, Nicolas de Staël, Gérard Garouste and Anselm Kiefer. In music, Bartók, Stravinsky and even the little *Piano Sonata* by Berg. These are basically the true inventors of post-deconstructionist art, of postmodern art, and this is what interests me these days. I'm not trying to say that everything in this particular story has been negative. I'm simply saying that, in the twentieth century, we had a story that was *mainly* that of deconstruction and innovation and that we now need to ask what comes after, in the twenty-first century. When are we finally going to bring together once more innovation and beauty, innovation and the great human experiences? The authors I've just mentioned already give us some idea of this. And this is precisely what I'm seeking, too, in the field of a philosophy that must also become post-deconstructionist.

Claude Capelier: There are still two ambiguities that we need to try and clear up. The first is this: in my view, it's difficult just from

the chronological point of view to place *The Rite of Spring*, composed in 1913, in the 'post-deconstructionist' period. It would be
fairer, I reckon, to say that Stravinsky managed to construct a
world on the basis of the dynamic of deconstruction of an innovation, while going beyond it. And this brings me to my second
point: when you say that Stravinsky, Bartók, Kundera and Roth
open the way to a 'post-deconstructionist' art, is this because you
really feel that they integrate dimensions liberated by the moderns
within a new and more profound perspective, or is it simply
because these are artists who have, in style and form, kept up some
'old-fashioned' modes of expression or composition?

Luc Ferry: In the case of Stravinsky, I have a doubt. I'm not sure
that a strict chronology is necessarily a good arbiter. Also, the
music of Schoenberg was already there, so it was already possible
to map one's own position in regard to it and then go further.
After all, in other fields, there have been geniuses who were incredibly in advance of their time. When Pico della Mirandola formulated the new principles of human dignity in 1486, he was
announcing word for word what Rousseau would repeat in the
middle of the eighteenth century. More simply, I think that with
The Rite of Spring, we have modern beauty, already a huge distance from the nineteenth century and yet, unlike Boulez or
Stockhausen, it's beautiful, so beautiful it takes your breath away.
I'm fully prepared to admit that the dissonances of Boulez can
have an 'effect' on the listener, but frankly, is 'beauty' the right
term? I admit this will be found a very subjective remark. But all
the same, while millions of people listen to and play Bach throughout the world, how many listen to Boulez? A few score, a few
hundred at most and, in my view, there's a reason for this – and
anyway, a great number of people admire him, correctly, as a
conductor much more than as a composer. Finally, even in terms
of chronology, Stravinsky lived into the 1970s – didn't he? – which
in spite of everything makes him our contemporary.
    These details aren't so important. What interests me are the
authors who invented a resolutely modern art, an art that
was clearly of their own age, and yet beautiful. Drawing on the
typology I mentioned at the beginning, I think that these musi-
cians, these novelists are in the 'fifth principle', the new vision
of humanity that has opened up with the revolution of love. This

is not deconstruction. However much I admire Nietzsche and Heidegger, I think that we're no more in the age of Nietzsche and Heidegger, philosophically speaking, than in that of Kant and Voltaire. The artists I'm citing here may be contemporaries of the century of deconstruction, but they themselves are already in the next era, that of the second humanism.

This is what I'd like to say, as it's the essential point revealed by an attentive and self-aware description of the relations that the works we are discussing may have with the vision of existence that is ours. If, with the revolution of love and philosophy that is mine, I could be in the least little way anything like a minor equivalent of Kundera or Roth, I'd have achieved my aim. This is obviously what I'm endeavouring to do, at my very modest level.

Art has always been the creation of a work, from some sensible material, to comprise a great representation of the world: this is the definition given by Hegel, and I think it's correct. Greek art, for example, is Greek cosmology embodied in stone, in statuary: the harmony of the faces, the proportion of the bodies and temples, is a sensible reflection of the idea of the cosmos. It's the cosmic harmony embodied in something material. Art is the embodiment of great ideas and great values in a sensible material that may be the sculptor's or architect's stone, the composer's sound vibrations, the painter's drawing or colour, and so on. This is what gives art its superiority over philosophy: it says the same thing as philosophy, but it says it in a way that is really touching, moving, sensible – and philosophical conceptual arguments cannot, of course, do this.

Just as there have been five great visions of the world, philosophically speaking, we have now entered a fifth era in the history of art. In literature, this is in my view already incarnated by authors such as Philip Roth or Milan Kundera. What deconstruction has made possible – this is true, and I happily concur with you – is the representation of new dimensions of the human. And, as I've said, Roth and Kundera describe old age, sex and love in a very different way from Stendhal and Balzac. It's not the same period. They go back to old elements that I like because we find a plot, a story and characters, but that's not why I am so excited about them: what I like is the way they make me sensitive and even sometimes reveal to me quite new points of view on dimensions of human life that have become the very fabric of our existences, but that nineteenth-century novelists ignored. When Philip Roth talks about his health problems, his difficulties in making love, his impotence, his cancer, but also about the politically correct in America, about feminism, and so on, he is describing like no one else the truth of the 'deconstructed' human: the human is no longer idealized, rationalized, seen as a clear conscience. It's contemporary human life in all its greatness and real wretchedness, experiences connected to a particular period and presenting us with a quite new palette of possibilities. You're right to say this is possible only after the century of deconstruction on every level which liberated, as we've said, the unconscious, sex, incoherence, the irrational and all that goes with this. That's what I find really new in these authors: in their works, we're no longer in the first humanism of reason and law, nor in pure deconstruction, but in what is a much wider and deeper approach to human being. This is what I like and I also find it, *mutatis mutandis*, in Ravel's *Concerto for the Left Hand* and in Bartók's violin concertos or, even though it is dated 1913, *The Rite of Spring*. It's not a question of strict chronology.

And what you said, over and above the examples, shows that our points of view are ultimately close to one another. The question is whether we have emerged from an art of deconstruction, from an art of innovation for innovation's sake, to enter an art that gives a different expression to the great human experiences, those of a wider, richer humanity, more varied and more emotional, in which more human elements are included.

Modern popular art has, like no other in history, been responsible for the spread of a new sensibility that is part of the revolution of love

Up until now we've been talking only of 'great art', of classical music and the plastic arts. But we shouldn't underestimate the fact that, in the twentieth century, new forms of expression developed in popular music. Something that I rather like, sometimes, in the tradition of rock (and we can now speak of traditions in rock), is precisely this: it played on new aspects of human subjectivity. One can also say that it's very elementary, that it's not as sophisticated as classical music, but all the same, when we're talking about the body, sex, seduction and the way we can move when we're dancing, this music has invented a great deal. There's not just the noble, 'classical' kind of dance, that of Béjart and Pina Bausch: there are also those kinds of dance that have liberated themselves and no longer resemble the Sissi waltz or the Auvergne bourrée. The way we started to dance, to move, in the 1960s, to music that had something highly sensual about it, was light years away from the way people danced in the time of Louis XV or at the Viennese court in the nineteenth century. These dimensions of the human that now lie at the heart of collective life, where they were once corseted by conventions or relegated to the boudoir, have been fostered by jazz and rock much more than by classical music. Just to speak my own mind and be a bit provocative, I have much more admiration for the Beatles or for Ray Charles or even for some songs by the Rolling Stones than I do for Boulez. They're so much more 'me'.

Claude Capelier: I'm full of admiration for the Beatles, but at the same time I think that Boulez is one of the greatest composers of all time – there's no incompatibility! Indeed, it's a characteristic of our time, the direct consequence of the way we now value more varied dimensions of existence: more and more of us are unhesitatingly open to all sorts of music, drama, and artistic expressions, from the most sophisticated to the most basic. Of course, nobody plays or listens to Stockhausen in the same way they play or listen to a pop video by Michael Jackson, but it's just this variety of experience that means we want to do both. It's possible to like Schoenberg and Rihanna, not because we think there's no difference and they're treated as equal, but, on the contrary because they give us quite different pleasures. What has also changed, in the wake of deconstruction and the revolution of love is that all the things which have been liberated are bound up with dimensions of life so consubstantial with human being that they are found everywhere, in the most demanding arts as much as in the coarsest expressions: nowadays, the objects and subjects are the same, but they are treated from points of view that are more or less highly developed and profound. This is particularly clear in the case of music: current songs play a great deal on the physical effect of sound, and so does contemporary classical music; but the former tend to remain content with this, while the latter adds several other strata. This common point entails others: the interpretation of early music has been profoundly marked, not just by Stravinsky, but also by rock and by jazz. These days, the conductors of altogether traditional orchestras tend, in their turn, to accelerate the tempi, to accentuate the music in much more marked ways, and give it a much more dancing rhythm than before. This physical effect of music has become very important for us. This, too, is the revolution of love.

Luc Ferry: I'm not at all pessimistic about what's happening now, or about the future. I simply think there was a kind of terrorism of deconstruction, especially in the 1950s, 1960s and even 1970s which hampered a great number of writers and artists who felt absolutely obliged to produce dissonance and difference, blank paintings or concerts of silence. But all that's over and I think that the revolution of love now has its artists and novelists of genius who give shape to hitherto forgotten dimensions of existence whose beauty we are discovering, and the meaning they help to embody in our lives.

Conclusion: Death, the Only Objection? Love, a Utopia?

By way of conclusion, I need to reply to two questions that I'm asked so often that they are, as it were, impossible to sidestep. So I mustn't even try to sidestep them!

The first is as easy to ask as it is difficult, or impossible, to answer: if love is what gives meaning to our lives, what are we to do about death, which brings it to a full stop? What's the point of loving if everything has to end one day, without any hope of returning? How can we fail to see that what claims to give meaning is, in these conditions, completely devoid of meaning?

The second question is equally redoubtable from the point of view of a philosophy of love: by suggesting that this latter, via the evolutions and revolutions in the modern family, am I not being excessively optimistic, or indeed boundlessly naive? Isn't it obvious that it is the most dismal passions that rule the world today: avidity, greed, hatred, jealousy and, to crown it all, a fierce individualistic egotism that has never been as violent and arrogant as it is these days? Isn't the idea of a 'politics of love' quite simply a bit ridiculous, given the harshness of current social and political realities?

The contradiction between love and death

That there is, between love and death, an intolerable contradiction has been known by mankind since the very beginning. The first book ever to be written in historical time, *The Epic of Gilgamesh*, composed in the eighteenth century BC in Sumerian, already bore witness to this: it is this theme, and no other, which it places at the heart of its plot. I have discussed this at length in *The Revolution of Love*. So I won't go over it again here, except to emphasize that the condition of modern man has made this contradiction even more acute, with the result that the first question, although asked *sub specie aeternitatis*, is probably more crucial today than ever before. We've seen how marrying for love had emerged when individuals broke away from village communities, religious in nature and consisting of peasants, where people married, if not under duress, at least without their opinion on the matter being in the least consulted. I've also said that this break was itself both the effect of the new wage-earning arrangements and the condition of the love match. But moving away from the village and into cities and factories where waged work would confer on individuals, especially women, a financial autonomy, enabling them to marry instead of being married by others – this distancing, in other words, was also a distancing from the weight of religions and thereby spelled out the lessening of religion's hold and even atheism and the secularization of the world. As a result, at the (provisional) end of this journey, the modern individual is *both less protected from the suffering of grief and more exposed than ever to its torments.*

In other words (but this boils down to the same thing), we are now more loving than ever, more bound than ever to those we love, to our children and our families, and simultaneously less protected than ever from grief by those great safety nets, the great religions. This is because, quite simply, we are less imbued with religious relief than in the past. Many people, even if they call themselves Christians, do not really believe in the resurrection of the dead, in the promise that we will be reunited with those we have loved in this life. Hence the presence of an indisputably tragic dimension in the condition of modern man. Hence also the fact that the theme of death – for example in the form of providing company for the dying, the right to die with dignity, euthanasia and assisted suicide – keeps cropping up in the debates that preoccupy secular society.

The fact of the matter is that, given the contradiction between love, which drives us to form attachments, and death, which is an intolerable (because irremediable) separation, the tradition of the great secular or religious spiritualities includes only two approaches, both of which are in my view quite unsatisfactory. First, there is the approach of the philosophers who, from the Stoics and the Epicureans up to Schopenhauer via the Buddhist thinkers, endeavour (unsuccessfully, in my view) to demonstrate that 'death is nothing for the wise', for those who have sufficiently trained their minds to grasp that it is not terrifying in comparison with the reality of the cosmos or of universal life. The second is the approach of religions, in particular Christianity which, not believing for a second in the benefits of philosophy, puts forward a 'real solution': it doesn't pretend that it's not afraid of the death of those we love, but it believes in the promise that we'll see them again, in a future life.

The first approach doesn't convince me. As for the second, its main drawback – rather a serious one – is that you need to have faith to believe in it.

The failure of the philosophies of death is clear ...

Indeed, as I have explained in *The Revolution of Love*, it is my view that none of the great philosophies, however admirable they may be, really answers the question that has been raised. They try rather to cloud the issue, to get round the difficulty by persuading us that we are mad to complain about such a necessary event – and one which is without importance since it concerns only our little selves. The problem is that the little self in question is the only one that we live in, the only one that is affected directly by its love and by its death. People explain to us that, from the point of view of universal life, of the species or the cosmos, our wretched individuality is only of very limited interest. But, if we think about it more deeply, we soon realize that our representations of life in general, of the species or of the cosmos in the name of which people would like to see our paltry 'concern for ourselves' fade away, are mere abstractions: it's difficult to see why their pseudo-reality, both universal and abstract, should prevail over the particular and concrete reality of the individual consciousness that suffers, loves and dies. As a result, the promises made in the name of these abstractions are ultimately worth rather little.

The pinnacle of this perfectly logical and totally unconvincing line of argument was probably attained, as we have seen, by Epicurus – and I doubt that he ever managed to convince a single human being on this earth. Epicurus told his disciples: 'Death is nothing for us, since as long as we are alive, death is not there, and when death is there, we no longer exist. So death is related neither to the living nor to the dead, since it does not exist for the former, and the latter no longer exist!' QED.

La Rochefoucauld, a Christian thinker happy at last to see the 'wrong answers' of philosophy being so clearly ruled out of court, puts it very eloquently in a passage quoted by my friend Denis Moreau in his fine book *Les Voies du salut* (*The Paths to Salvation*, 2010):

> Nothing proves more how fearful death is than the efforts the philosophers make to persuade us to despise it... It is reasonable to say something about the falseness of the contempt for death. I hear about this contempt for death that the pagans boast of deriving from their own strength ... And the weakest men, as well as heroes, have left us with countless celebrated examples to support this opinion. And yet I doubt whether anyone sensible has ever believed it. And the efforts one makes to persuade other people, as well as oneself, of its truth show quite clearly that this endeavour is not easy.

Fundamentally, I share the view of Jacques Derrida, which tends the same way as La Rochefoucauld's opinion; his admission is especially moving since, when he was expressing his thoughts in an interview with *Le Monde*, he was fighting the cancer that would kill him a few months later:

> Learning to live should mean learning to die, learning to accept, so as to take into account, absolute mortality (that is, without salvation, resurrection, or redemption – neither for oneself nor for the other). That's been the old philosophical injunction since Plato: to philosophize is to learn to die. I believe in this truth without being able to resign myself to it. And less and less so. I have never learned to accept it, to accept death, that is. [...] I remain uneducable when it comes to any kind of wisdom about knowing-how-to-die or, if you prefer, knowing-how-to-live. I have still not learned or picked up anything on this subject.[1]

Hence, of course, the temptation of religion.

---

[1] Jacques Derrida, *Learning to Live Finally: The Last Interview*, trans. Pascale-Anne Brault and Michael Naas (London: Palgrave Macmillan, 2007), pp. 24–5.

The temptation of religion

So, we need to acknowledge that the great religions, unlike philosophy, do at least have the merit of confronting the question raised, not evading it or tackling it merely indirectly. They give it a solution that lives up to its demands. Without beating about the bush, Christianity promises us *exactly* what we want to hear: the resurrection of souls and bodies. And to crown it all, it assures us that we will be able to see again, after death, in another life, those whom we love in this one. How can we resist? To escape from our fears, to ensure that we can make 'death itself die' and thus enable humans beings to love without anxiety or restraint, four conditions need to be met, as believers have understood full well and as Denis Moreau sets out in a perfectly rigorous way: 'Death must not be the end; there must be a persistence of personal identity after death; there must be a relative heterogeneity between the form of being that we know now and that experienced after death; and we must be allowed to hope that this post mortem continuation can occur in relatively felicitous, or indeed very felicitous, conditions.'

In other words, we will be fully serene and reassured only if we are certain that another life will take over once we have died, a life in which we will remain fully ourselves, real individual persons, with our own souls and bodies. Of course, this new life must be rather different from that old one; above all, it must be happier, much happier, since death will no longer have any place and love will reign supreme. What an amazing coincidence! – This is what Christ promises to those who follow him. And of course, as can easily be imagined, this promise of personal resurrection causes a complete upheaval in the concrete reality of the Christian's existential attitude. Perhaps I may quote Moreau again:

> The believer's life is a life characterized by faith in the resurrection of Christ and by the hope in his or her own resurrection. If we take this faith and this hope seriously, they are not something that you might have in parallel with other ideas, as an ornament or consolation for life, but they define the Christian's whole being and place him in a specific relation with the world that modifies his being in the world.

From this point of view, indeed, philosophy is of little help. Only religion can give us true salvation which resides of course in the 'death of death' itself and not just in any self-proclaimed but fallacious victory over the fear it arouses. The main difficulty – though not the only one, as I shall go on to show – is that one needs to believe in it, to have faith, that unshakeable faith – *fides* – in Jesus' words, in his promised 'good news' (*evangelium* or gospel) of the resurrection of bodies and a meeting after death.

This is for each person to decide. But if we do not have faith, and if philosophy is not much help (on this precise point of course, not on all the others), how are we to deal with the contradiction between love and death?

Another approach to the question: meaning 'in' life instead of the meaning 'of' life

I'm not going to claim to have *the* solution, which would be very arrogant and probably way beyond my abilities. Faced with the loss of those I love, I don't feel any better prepared than was Derrida at the prospect of his own death. Probably less, in fact: our death doubtless fills us with anxiety, and sometimes dread, but when confronted with the death of other people, especially our children, grief can quite simply overwhelm us, flatten us, and the sense of absolute meaninglessness can in the twinkling of an eye disarm the most sophisticated reasons. I'd be the last to deny this and the last to claim that I am above the common run of mortals in this regard.

What I tell myself, and what I tell my friends when I see them suffering, is that love is still worthwhile. Indeed, it is even more worthwhile – worth all the pain, and the joy, too. All stories come to an end; there is no doubt about that. Should we for all that give up, not read a book again because we will one day reach the final page, not listen to a chorale by Bach because the last note will soon be sounding, not watch a film because *The End* is written across the last image? Not only can I not accept the Christian message because I do not have faith, but it seems to me still a bit too inclined to make this human life here and now a mere preamble to the beyond, a painful propaedeutic to another life, fuller, more serene, more joyful. If this is the truth, fine, but if it's just an illusion, if in reality there's just one single life, the one we live on this earth, there's a great risk of our being not saved for eternity but quite simply definitely deluded. In this regard, Pascal's famous wager is no more convincing in my view than the argument of Epicurus.

It's here that the difference between the meaning 'of' life and meaning 'in' life seems relevant. Life – unless seen from a religious point of view where we imagine we could place ourselves as it were outside it, from the point of view of the beyond – probably has no meaning. It is nonetheless, like a novel, like a chorale by Bach, if envisaged from the viewpoint of the direct relation we have with it, full of meaning and value, and it would be crazy to deprive ourselves of these just because they will one day be lost.

This is why, when faced with the loss of someone we love, a loss that we all experience sooner or later, I tell myself that, so long as there is still someone in this world to love, so long as love, a real or even just a possible love, exists in this world, it is still worth living. We sometimes think, when faced with a loss or even a separation, when the loved person leaves us one way or another, that it's all over, that the absolute and total catastrophe that we foresaw and feared all along, has finally happened and that it's going to annihilate us. Two or three years later, sometimes less, we realize that this is not so, that there are still things in life to experience, people to love.

Don't think that I'm here being excessively optimistic or frivolous: I know that it can happen in the life of a human being that he or she really has nothing more to hope for. But this is rare. Most of the time there is new love; someone else is there, next to us, and if there is any saying in Christianity that should be preserved, it's the one that is as deep as the sea and is so rarely understood – the one enjoining us to 'leave the dead to bury the dead'. However, this presupposes (and this brings me to the second question) that we fully realize that we can build into this life, the only one granted to us in my view, a real wisdom of love. At the personal level, of course, where the moral question, that of mere respect for the other person, yields to a myriad of questions arising from what may be called, in the sense I have said, spiritual life – in which, it also seems to me, philosophy, while it cannot really declare death to be dead any more than the religions do, still has an irreplaceable finality to it: how can we live from day to day with those we love while knowing that no sooner has a person been born than he or she is old enough to die? How are we to make them as happy as possible? How are we to avoid or settle conflicts? How, as we have discussed, are we to raise our children? How much transparency should there be in a couple? How are we to transform the romantic love that lasts for only a short while into a more enduring tenderness or loving friendship?

It is also at the collective level that love needs to find its place. How can we get human beings to live together given that, as I've mentioned, they are creatures of passion rather than ruled by their interests? What place can fraternity and sympathy, those collective derivatives of love, occupy in the public space? And isn't this space, contrary to what I've been saying in this very book, thereby siding with the naive, the place of the most dismal passions, much more than it is a world in which love would have its place?

Ethics and politics of love: towards a new categorical imperative

Indeed, if we are to believe some people, our societies have never been less egalitarian, more 'individualistic' and uncaring about the weak than is the case today. Every day, new voices arise to condemn it: 'Look at the bonuses paid to city traders, the profits of the banks, the deporting of immigrants, the racism and the xenophobia, the arrogance of the rich towards the poverty of the unemployed. Equality, fraternity – you bet! What we need is a change of direction, a revolution to destroy the current order.' This always guarantees a round of applause from the left-wing seats in the National Assembly.

There is just one thing: this type of language rests entirely on a historically and factually incorrect, not to say absurd, analysis. Contrary to the usual stereotypes, unthinkingly parroted, about our societies being riddled with 'individualism' – a term confused with a vague notion of selfishness – the truth is that societies have never been more solicitous towards people, more intent on their rights and their well-being, than our old democracies. I must insist on this point: nowhere else and at no other period have people taken more care of others. I defy anyone to prove the opposite, to show a single example in a real society, either in history or in geography, that had – whether in a recession or nor – protected not just its own citizens, but foreigners too, even illegal immigrants (let me note in passing that the law obliges us all to educate all foreign children, whatever the situation – legal or illegal – of the parents), that created a more powerful and more efficient welfare state than the one from which we all benefit from the moment we are born.

Who will deny that this isn't enough – but can anything, by definition, be enough in this domain? – or that inequalities grow in a period of recession? But when and where has anyone done any better? I'd like to know! As André Comte-Sponville writes, quite correctly, in his *Le Goût de vivre*:

> Some people hope that with the recession, 'we're going to get back to a bit more generosity, a bit less selfishness'. This is because they haven't understood a thing about economics, or about humankind. Heavens above – what are we to go back to, and when? Do you think that nineteenth-century society was more generous and less selfish than ours? Re-read Balzac and Zola! And in the seventeenth century? Re-read Pascal, La Rochefoucauld, Molière! In the Middle Ages? Re-read the historians! In antiquity? Re-read Tacitus, Suetonius, Lucretius! Selfishness is not a new idea.

It could hardly be put any better. Of course, we need to appeal to the ideal in order to criticize the real – to natural law to contrast it with positive law: that's obvious. But we still need to indicate which reality we are talking about and in the name of which ideal we are acting. And as it happens, in spite of all the defects that will be found in it, the reality in our welfare states is quite simply the gentlest, most humane, the most protective that has ever been known in human history. As for the ideal in the name of which its defects are criticized, I may be permitted to doubt, now and always, that the cracked old refrain of Maoism and Trotskyism, those doctrines that have invariably led to the worst human catastrophes wherever they were imposed on peoples, is these days in any better position to do any better than this admirable blend of liberty and well-being that our democratic republics have managed to provide us with. Our standard of living, whatever we may choose to say of it, is these days, on average, three times higher in France than it was in my childhood. You need only travel to Africa, India, China or even Latin America to gauge the extent to which, in spite of all the legitimate criticisms we may make of our democracies, the latter are incredibly privileged when it comes to legal and social protection. Although it is difficult for the (many) people who complacently wallow in resentment and negativity to admit it, our world is far less harsh than in the past. They never stop harping on about the anxieties of young people; commonplace remarks can rain on our heads like cudgels but that doesn't make them any truer. Was it any easier to be twenty years old in 1914, in the Germany of the 1930s or indeed of the 1950s, when young men had to go off to Algeria? The last world war left over fifty million dead – a sum total of grief for every family that is almost unimaginable today. The baby boom generation will have been the first in our modern history not to experience war. Isn't this huge progress?

I don't see that it would be naive to think and write that, yes, there's no denying it, our modern European societies are the first in which feelings of fraternity and sympathy, which are simply offshoots of the principle of love in the collective sphere, have managed to become embodied in reality, taking institutional shape in a welfare state which past centuries had not the least idea of and which the rest of the world envies – as is indeed proved by the pattern of migration which invariably goes from south to north, not the other way round. And if our societies these days, as some unthinking '*indignados*' proclaim, are threatened by regression, this is not at all because they are led by crazed liberals whose plan, which they do not and dare not admit to, is to destroy public services and social welfare, but because the BRIC countries, the new entries, starting with China, impose on our societies the burden of a triple dumping – social, economic and monetary – that I mentioned above.

Hence, too, the fact that there is nothing comic or absurd in reflecting on moral action, and even political action, in terms of love. We simply need to adopt a new formulation of what Kant called the categorical imperative.

Let's make this a bit clearer.

A new categorical imperative: 'Act in such a way that you can desire to see the decisions you take being applied also to the people you love most'

This is what I called, in *La Sagesse des modernes*, a 'politics of love'. I used this phrase in opposition to André Comte-Sponville who, as an heir to Marx and Hobbes, defended instead, as I mentioned above, a politics of interests. I think, unlike Hobbes or Marx, that politics would benefit from thinking more in terms of sympathy and fraternity.

From this viewpoint, the formula of a new imperative could be more or less the following: 'Act in such a way that the maxim of your action could be applied to those whom you love the most.' If I think about this more deeply, it strikes me that, if we conformed to such a maxim, we would treat foreigners or the unemployed differently from the way we do. Imagine they are our own children. ... 'Act in such a way that the maxim of your action can be universalized for all those whom you love', not as a law of Nature, in Kant's way, but as a law of Love. If we examined every political decision using this measure, this criterion of selection might yield very different results from those we usually choose – especially because such an imperative inevitably brings with it an absolute demand for equity. When we see a former prime minister changing his son's rent with a stroke of his pen because he has power over the apartments in the city of Paris,[2] I'm not going to be the one to throw the first stone, but I'd simply ask him: what about the others? I say this in all sincerity: the educational reforms that I put in motion when I was minister (repeating the same class if you failed exams in primary schools, sandwich classes, operation *Desire to Act* that aimed to help young people realize and enhance their plans for selfless activities in a sort of prefiguration of civic service that I was able to set up in the ministry), I chose them, as I suggested above, on the basis of a criterion that was very clear to my eyes: if this reform had to be applied to my own children, would I decide to implement it or not? This doesn't mean that I was making reforms on their behalf, of course, but that the bond between the collective and the private was not broken. It's no longer a matter, as Kant thought, of acting 'according to that maxim whereby you can, at the same time, will that it should become a universal law', but 'in such a way that the decisions you take are such that you can wish to see them being applied to the people you love the most'. In my view, this is an excellent compass – the best there is in politics.

---

[2] This was one allegation brought against Alain Juppé. He was found guilty in 2004 of misuse of public funds.

Is this utopian? Probably: but this utopia, unlike those that were applauded in May 1968 at a time when blood was being shed for them throughout the world, is an exclusively constructive utopia and, given the way it is constructed, not death-dealing.

Let's take this further. I'd say that, in this new formulation of the categorical imperative, that of the second humanism, the latter seems as far removed from the first as the words of Jesus, in the Sermon on the Mount (Matthew 5:17–20), were from the Ten Commandments and the legalist orthodoxy of his time. When he said 'Think not that I am come to destroy the law [...] but to fulfil' it, he was clearly alluding to the logic of law. I suggest this parallel, with all due reverence, of course, because in both cases what we have is a shift from Law to love, the move from a purely legal categorical imperative to a categorical imperative linked to the sense of fraternity and sympathy.

Hegel devoted some really sublime words to this shift in a short youthful essay (unfortunately, it's fearsomely difficult) called *The Spirit of Christianity and its Fate*. Although his interpretation of Judaism is reductive and false, he does give us a magisterial commentary on the Sermon on the Mount, in particular the statement by Jesus that I've just mentioned which was aimed against the Orthodox Jews, the Pharisees and Sadducees: 'Think not that I have come to destroy the law [...] but to fulfil [it]. [...] For I say unto you, That except your righteousness shall exceed the righteousness of the scribes and Pharisees, ye shall in no case enter into the Kingdom of Heaven.' It is these words of Christ that Hegel contrasts both to Judaism and Kantianism: while in Judeo-Kantian morality the Law is imposed from on high on our natural inclinations, on our selfish inclinations, like a transcendent imperative, it is, in Christianity, love which, in some degree working upwards, brings about the accomplishment or, as it were, 'fulfilment' (in Greek, *pleroma*) of the Law: there is no need for a 'thou shalt!', of an imperative command or a duty falling from on high, for a mother to realize that she needs to give her breast to her child when it is hungry. So it's not a matter of destroying the Law but rather of fulfilling it and, in fulfilling it through love, its imperative form is suppressed. The form of the Law disappears, but the demand that it brought with it is still there: that is what Jesus meant. Thus love transcends the split between the particular and the universal, between nature and spirit. It was in this sense that, in the Sermon on the Mount, Jesus took up one after another the Ten Commandments – he says explicitly that he will not change a letter of them, not a jot – in such a way as to show that, in the form of commands (of imperatives, i.e., in so far as they are not carried out by love), they are worthless. Hegel writes: 'Against such commands [as "Thou shalt not kill"] Jesus sets virtue, i.e., a loving disposition, which makes the content of the command superfluous and destroys its form as a command.'[3] In short, love makes the Law superfluous as law, not because it rejects its message but on the contrary because it embodies it without having to make it into a transcendent categorical imperative. With Christianity, the religion of division and of unhappiness is thus overcome.

In the same way, I'd say that the first humanism was a humanism of Law and reason. It was that of the Enlightenment and the rights of man, of the French republicans and of Kant. The second is a humanism of fraternity and sympathy. If we take it seriously, it changes the whole situation. It is like a secularized homage to Jesus' message, an echo of the fact that, at the time when this message was given, it must have appeared like a flash of lightning in a clear sky, like a radical utopia. Although it is secularized, or rather because it is, and this secularization has enabled the many different dimensions of the human to blossom, the second humanism is now the only vision of the world borne by the breath of a utopia that, perhaps for the first time, does not threaten us with new catastrophes. For the ideal that it is aiming to bring about is no longer that of Nation or Revolution. It is no longer a question of organizing great massacres in the name of those deadly principles that supposed themselves to be outside and above humanity, but of preparing the future of those we love the most, and thus of future generations.

---

[3] Hegel, 'The Spirit of Christianity and its Fate', in *Early Theological Writings*, tr. T. M. Knox (Chicago: University of Chicago Press, 1975), pp. 182–301; p. 215.

Index